A SE
THE POEMS

Other books by Laura (Riding) Jackson from Persea

First Awakenings: The Early Poems of Laura Riding

The Poems of Laura Riding: A New Edition of the 1938 Collection

Selected Poems: In Five Sets

Progress of Stories

The Word "Woman" and Other Related Writings

Four Unposted Letters to Catherine

A Selection of the Poems of Laura Riding

Edited, with an introduction by

Robert Nye

PERSEA BOOKS
New York

Persea Books, Inc.
171 Madison Avenue
New York, New York 10016

Library of Congress Cataloging-in-Publication Data

Riding, Laura, 1901–
[Poems. Selections]
A selection of the poems of Laura Riding / edited with an
introduction by Robert Nye.
p.   cm.
Includes index.
ISBN 0-89255-221-2 (alk. paper)
I. Nye, Robert.   II. Title.
PS3519.A363A6   1996
811'.52—dc20   96-14741
                                                CIP

To Elizabeth Friedmann

Contents

Introduction

When the true history of twentieth-century poetry in the English language comes to be written, I believe that the poems of Laura Riding—and the story that goes with them—will be seen to be as important as anything in it.

The first thing to grasp about this poet is the threefold nature of her name. Born Laura Reichenthal in New York in 1901, she gave herself the name of Laura Riding when she began writing the poems of her major accomplishment, becoming Laura (Riding) Jackson when she stopped. In her early years in America she was for a brief while associated with the Fugitives, that group of poets which included John Crowe Ransom and Allen Tate; they gave her a prize for her work in 1924. At the end of 1925 she came to England, where her first book of poems, *The Close Chaplet*, was published by the Hogarth Press a year later, and she began a personal and literary association with Robert Graves which lasted until 1939. At that point, or soon after, having returned to America, she renounced the writing of poetry. In 1941 she married Schuyler Jackson, another ex-poet and a scholar of the neglected English writer Charles Doughty; together they worked for many years on a monumental book on language entitled *Rational Meaning: A New Foundation for the Definition of Words*. She published her 'personal evangel', *The Telling*, over her later life name of Laura (Riding) Jackson in 1972. She died in Florida, on 2 September 1991, at the age of ninety, having been awarded the Bollingen Prize earlier that year for her lifelong services to poetry.

During the twenty years or so of her active poethood, Laura Riding said several things about the nature of poetry which illuminate not just poetry itself but her own practice of it. One of the most memorable and arresting comes at the beginning of her book of essays entitled *Contemporaries and Snobs* (1928), where she declares: 'There is a sense of life so real that it becomes the sense of something more real than life . . . It is the meaning at work in what has no meaning; it is, at its clearest, poetry.' A decade later, introducing her *Collected Poems* (1938), she referred to a poem as 'an uncovering of truth of so fundamental and general a kind that no other name besides poetry is adequate except truth.' Both definitions bespeak a seriousness regarding the poetic vocation which might be rated rare in any century. Both definitions also bespeak a

1

faith in poetry so high, intense and whole-hearted that Laura Riding's silence as a poet after a certain point could be imagined to betoken a mystery. Laura (Riding) Jackson herself did her incomparable best to explain that mystery, and the reader is referred to her writings on the subject, all of them of the profoundest interest. Basically, she seems to have come to the conclusion that there was nowhere further for her (or indeed anyone else) to go with or through poem-writing; she believed that poetry itself was exhausted, that it had run out of possibilities, or rather that it stood revealed as never having truly possessed those possibilities for a complete propriety of word to thought which it had seemed to have in the hopes of its adherents. In a word, this writer hailed by Martin Seymour-Smith in his *Who's Who in Twentieth-Century Literature* (1976) as 'the most consistently good woman poet of all time' decided that the practice of poetry is truth-baffling, that its procedures make it impossible for it to fulfill the linguistic and spiritual expectations which it excites. Respecting this decision as one must, I would still remark that Laura Riding's poems seem to me to express what would be otherwise inexpressible, saying that which could not be said were it not for the moment of the poem and the medium of poetry. Her finest poems, moreover, seem to me those in which she makes discovery as she writes, poems in which the heart's and mind's truth comes more as something learned than something taught. Prose may be the medium for those who know what they mean before they say it, whereas in poetry there is never quite that degree of intention, the meaning being what the poet finds in the act of writing. Laura (Riding) Jackson's published post-poetic explanations of her own poems and her reasons for not writing more of them after 1939 leave out of account the involuntary nature of the poetic genius which she undoubtedly possessed.

Laura Riding's voice, as it speaks and sings in the poems of her major inspiration and accomplishment, has always sounded to my ears as an essentially *English* voice.* This is in part because the

---

*This has to do with language, not nationality. 'A literature is the literature of a language', as C. H. Sisson has it, and 'one does not think of St. Augustine as an African writer, of Seneca or Martial as Spanish writers. . . .' The observation comes in the essay 'Some Reflections on American Literature' in his volume *In Two Minds: Guesses at Other Writers* (1990).

poems are so well-spoken, so well-sung, so exquisitely scrupulous in their use of the English language. Yet perhaps such essential Englishness comes equally from the way the poet chose from the start to address her own originality to the matter of tradition:

> As well as any other, Erato,
> I can dwell separately on what we know
> In common secrecy,
> And celebrate the old, adoréd rose,
> Retell—oh why—how similarly grows
> The last leaf of the tree.
>
> But for familiar sense what need can be
> Of my most singular device or me,
> If homage may be done
> (Unless it is agreed we shall not break
> The patent silence for mere singing's sake)
> As well by anyone?
>
> Mistrust me not, then, if I have begun
> Unwontedly and if I seem to shun
> Unstrange and much-told ground:
> For in peculiar earth alone can I
> Construe the word and let the meaning lie
> That rarely may be found.

This, from *The Close Chaplet*, is prosodically perfect, yet at the same time new and memorable in rhythm, the diction precise, the verbal shape unforced but urgent, the thought and feeling at one and as one truthful. It might be noticed how the rhyme draws out the sense in the regular variation between a three-stress and a five-stress iambic line, reflecting the measured regret of what is being said as well as the poet's fine firmness of purpose. Everything in the poem rises towards the word *construe*—an impassioned progress, lyrically anti-lyrical, beautifully appropriate in a poem addressed to the muse of lyric love poetry. *Construe*, though, is a very sharp word to find at the heart of a song. It pricks the mind into remembrance that meaning is all, and that for this poet nothing but heart-felt final meaning finally matters. Erato, I trust, could not be displeased by that. For the rest of us, any poet of the past six centuries would have been justly proud to have written the lines, but perhaps only a supremely modern poet with a knowl-

3

edge of the shortcomings of tradition and the burden of past perfections could have tried.

Regarding this matter of the Englishness of Laura Riding's poetic voice, some other lines inevitably come to mind:

> This posture and this manner suit
> Not that I have an ease in them
> But that I have a horror
> And so stand well upright—
> Lest, should I sit and, flesh-conversing, eat,
> I choke upon a piece of my own tongue-meat.

That is a whole poem, wittily entitled 'Grace'. The wit, I insist, is English, harking back to the satires of John Donne, and its peculiar veridical expression gave example and encouragement to a number of excellent English poets—Robert Graves, Norman Cameron and James Reeves among them. Even those critics who have missed the merits of her own work have usually been willing to grant Laura Riding's influence on others. There is something of an academic consensus on this particular matter, though few or none seem to get it right when required to discuss precisely the nature of that influence, or its substance. What did these poets learn from Laura Riding, even where their work is not much like hers, and less like each other's than is commonly supposed? Not tricks or treats, I reckon, but a passion for exactness. These were the contemporaries who first tasted the purity of language to be found in her poems from the start, and who were at best moved by it to thirst for some similar depth and grace of expression in themselves. From the moment when her first published poem, 'Dimensions', appeared in *The Fugitive* in the autumn of 1923, what was being offered was a well-spring of the purest verbal lucidity, poems as clear and exact in their thinking and feeling as they are fresh and explicit in their speaking voice. As for her notorious 'difficulty', if you read the poems of Laura Riding slowly and carefully, referring back to the original meaning of any words that fall unexpectedly within them, then in my experience you will be startled into wonder at their simplicity. With language this good, all that is needed is your full and then your fullest attention. All that is required by way of guide and companion to a reading of these poems is the twelve-volume *Oxford English Dictionary*, and

4

its supplements, not because she uses lots of unusual words but because she doesn't.

For my own part, if a personal testimony may be allowed, I have loved these poems since I first discovered them, seemingly by accident, certainly at no one's direction, when I was about thirteen years old. This would have been a year or two after the discovery that I could get three tickets at the public library for each member of my family, but use them all myself, since none of the others was much of a reader. In this fashion, following nothing but my own nose, I read my way through all the volumes of English poetry that I could lay hands on, as well as several kinds of more eccentric and occult writing of strong appeal at that age when you are half-looking for a miracle which will serve to get you back in touch with your first remembered stirrings of consciousness. Here, so it seemed to me, finding that magical *Collected Poems* as it were hidden at the heart of the library, was poetry *absolute,* the culmination of all the volumes which I had been searching through. I had no idea who this woman called Laura Riding was, but to my mind and ear she had to be the one twentieth-century poet who started where the mighty voices of the past left off, and who then proceeded to take poetry to its extreme, and perhaps further. Her poems struck me (though I could not have said so) as a complete embodiment of grace of word and spirit. They were her mind, and reading them was to follow the process of her thought without interference. Individual poems possessed and expressed a singular beauty, separate lines and passages had a power of impressing themselves unforgettably upon the heart, but it was as a whole that the poems stood and required to be known, and it was as a whole that I came to revere them. Did I understand those poems then? Perhaps not. Sometimes, I confess, they seemed to me like spells, intimate and potent and precise invocations of matters beyond my intellectual and emotional grasp. And yet there is a sense in which the mind of a child more readily entertains such mysteries. For whatever reason, or for reasons beyond reason, as the words and their rhythms worked upon and then within me, I found in due course that here were not so much spells as acts of verbal *dis*enchantment, inspired unravellings of the world's riddle. Over the years since, I have never found these poems wanting in their account of how it is, essentially, with a result that now I might claim not just to believe them true but to know them truthful. Here is poetry as an articulation of the most exquisite consciousness, poetry as completely wakeful existence realised in words, with at the end of it the news that even poetry will not do. Here is work that reads the person reading it.

I first wrote to Laura Riding in the summer of 1962, when I made her a bold gift of my first book of poems. She acknowledged it with proper criticism of the boldness and the poems besides, I responded, and there followed four years of the most generous, intensive, and (for me) instructive correspondence, at the height of which I was given the honour of typing a fair copy of *The Telling* from her first draft. Our friendship was the most precious thing I knew, but it seemed to come to a sudden end in the autumn of 1966, when there were changes in my life which led to estrangement. My devotion to her poems never changed. In 1989 I wrote to her again, asking her permission to include some of her work in an anthology. Refusing, she addressed me kindly, and our correspondence was resumed. We met for the first time in the summer of 1991, at her home in Wabasso, on Florida's east coast, whither I had travelled at her request, being enabled to do so by a Society of Authors Travel Scholarship which came unasked-for just when it was needed. At the end of our first meeting she gave me copies of the typescripts of all her early unpublished poems which had been lost for years, and I sat up for most of the following night reading them in my motel room. Next morning, back at the little wooden house among the pine-trees, when I was trying to make sense of my excitement regarding these poems, stammering my way from one image to another in an attempt to define what I felt about them, she smiled and said, 'Write a poem about this, will you?' I said that I would do my best not to, which made her smile the more. There followed three days of the most extraordinary talk— about life, about death, about love, about poetry. It was not all high-flown, but her verbal exactitude was the same for the seemingly trivial as for the manifestly momentous, as when (in the first case) her nurse made us a chocolate pudding and she pronounced it pleasing to the taste but 'pebbly', or when (in the second) she took care to explain to me that there was a difference between Spinoza's saying 'God is an intellectual thing' and her own preferred formulation, 'The *name* God is an intellectual thing.' Meaning, she said, was the truly intellectual thing in poetry; 'its divinity, its deity, so to speak.' She remarked that in Doughty's poetry it is the single word that is important, whereas in her own

6

work it would be more sensible and appropriate to consider an excitement relative to the meaning of *all* the words. Of Robert Graves, the harshest criticism she allowed herself to express in my hearing was that he had been 'clumsy', but she said also that she thought that Thomas Hardy had proved himself 'an innocent' when he met Graves. Her eyes, which were blue as her gaze was straight and unwavering, lit up with pleasure when I mentioned Norman Cameron, and when I began telling her about my friend C. H. Sisson, supposing that she might not know his work, she surprised me by exclaiming instantly, 'Oh, but I like him! He's *serious*.' I shall never forget how at one point, after we had been talking of the ancient idea of the Great Chain of Being, she called me back urgently into her room to tell me that the real Great Chain of Being consisted of poets. 'Poets inspire poets,' she said. 'From here in this room to Homer, the Great Chain of Being stretches back.' She referred me also in this regard to the Ion in the *Dialogues* of Plato. She asked me to write about her poems, and I promised her that I would. Her accent, I should put it here on record, was so thoroughly anglicised, and her manner of speaking so pure in intonation, that at least one of the nurses in attendance had presumed her to be English before being assured that it was otherwise. All the time, in her every word, in her least gesture, I had the overwhelming sense that here was the poet who had written the songs of a modern Sappho more than fifty years before. Laura Riding and Laura (Riding) Jackson were one voice.

On the morning of the last day of my visit, she wrote a poem in her head which she then spoke to me and to her friend and biographer Elizabeth Friedmann as we sat together by her bedside:

> Oh love, love, love
> Moves the universe impressively
> In softened notes inaudibly close
> To silence.

Three weeks later, Laura (Riding) Jackson's heart stopped.

Of the work of all the poets I can think of, the work of Laura Riding is without doubt the least suitable or amenable to the kind of reduction attempted in this book. Her poems are one poem, and they ought to be read whole, either in that original *Collected Poems* of 1938, or in the new edition of the same book published by

7

Persea Books in 1980. The latter is still in print, and has the advantage also of providing Laura (Riding) Jackson's own account of why she renounced the writing of poems not long after preparing the first volume for the press. Since at the same time it includes as an appendix that soaring-spirited preface 'To the Reader' which introduced the 1938 book—an apology for and defence of poetry as good as anything on similar lines by Sidney or Shelley—this is probably the best place for any new reader to begin a serious study of the whole. Yet I hope that there is room for such a book as this one, if only to put into public use a possible key to an unlocking of the *Collected*. I know readers who recognize that there is great treasure here to be unlocked, but who have been discouraged from reading the poems as poems by their own failure to understand either Laura Riding's advocacy of poetry in the days of her poethood or her renunciation of poetry in the later time. Such readers must be respected, and may even be helped to find their own way into her work by what might amount to another reader's mistakes.

More could be said regarding the fact that so many of Laura Riding's poems are poems about love. However, I want now to let these poems speak for themselves. This book, which you hold in your hands, is what its title says it is—*A* selection of the poems of Laura Riding. The principle on which it is based is simple: I have included only those poems which I find I know by heart, either whole or in part, without ever having made any conscious effort to consign them to memory. The first eighteen poems come from *First Awakenings: The Early Poems of Laura Riding* (Persea Books, 1992). The poem here entitled 'Nor Is It Written' is the third of the 'Three Sermons to the Dead' in the *Collected Poems;* I feel able thus to present these great lines on their own since Laura Riding did so herself in Michael Roberts' *The Faber Book of Modern Verse* (1936).

Robert Nye
Cork, Ireland

Dimensions

Measure me for a burial
That my low stone may neatly say
In a precise, Euclidean way
How I am three-dimensional.

Yet can life be so thin and small?
Measure me in time. But time is strange
And still and knows no rule or change
But death and death is nothing at all.

Measure me by beauty.
But beauty is death's earliest name
For life, and life's first dying, a flame
That glimmers, an amaranth that will fade
And fade again in death's dim shade.

Measure me not by beauty, that fears strife.
For beauty makes peace with death, buying
Dishonor and eternal dying
That she may keep outliving life.

Measure me then by love – yet, no,
For I remember times when she
Sought her own measurements in me,
But fled, afraid I might foreshow
How broad I was myself and tall
And deep and many-measured, moving
My scale upon her and thus proving
That both of us were nothing at all.

Measure me by myself
And not by time or love or space
Or beauty. Give me this last grace:
That I may be on my low stone
A gage unto myself alone.
I would not have these old faiths fall
To prove that I was nothing at all.

Ceremonial

I shall bow three times
    In meeting.
I shall hate you correctly
    For greeting.

I shall kiss you each night,
    Proper and cool.
I shall keep my tongue neat and dry
    Your love to befool.

I shall polish my smile,
    Saluting your banners
With trim amiability
    And courteous manners.

I shall bow three times
    When we part,
Having murdered politely
    Your heart.

Conclusion

Some part of me is ever away
Faring in fields where something grows –
There's nowhere any but me that knows
The terrible herb I press each day
Into a bitter that never ran
So savory in another man.

What absent mood that keeps me fed
And moves the heart within the brute
Will one day gather the last root
And I'll be hungering and dead
Because some part of me comes back
Without the healing draught I lack?

When none of me can live to roam,
The wandering witch in me that found
A dram abroad to keep me sound
May yet discover a weed at home
To nourish and revive the rest
Of that in me I never guessed.

The Sweet Ascetic

Find me the thing to make me less
Delivered to my earthliness,
Some rarer love to live upon,
A berry grown in Avalon,
Something that will, in this emprise,
Suffice me to etherealize
The coarser strain and purify
The flesh that had preferred to die.

Find me this thing and plant it near
My garden gate so that some day,
When I am going out of it,
I'll stoop to pick the ripest bit
And, humming as I walk away,
Smile just a little and disappear.

To a Proud Lover

Until you have beheld her truly,
All she is,
The white wonder,
Out to the last prospect of her mysterious mind,
You cannot have her.

Her loving can but be
Your love's best vision of her
When the black bulbs
Will be unlidded, sprout sight.

Love is no invasion.
Do but comprehend, where you stand,
That her head is amplified in air,
That her hands include what they touch,
Lose not what they drop.
Under her the earth's appulse
Knots her with an infinite,
With what is next.

There is no need to laugh when she laughs,
There is no need to look where her eyes leap,
To accompany her.
There is no way to win her with art.
Care would be clumsy, even sinful.
Do but see simply the white wonder she is,
The many bright musics,
The appearance symphonic.

Yet how can you ever
Traverse your swart soul?
Bloom her freely enough
From your unfraught bulbs
That beblack and screen her candor,
Bebarren the all-implicit vision?

To see her purely
Who can see but darkly,
You must see her not at all,
You must have her not at all.

Unpour your pride.
Bid the very vessel thin,
Shred to receive her
As light not liquid,
As the pervading grace
Of your destruction
In the possession.

An Ancient Revisits

They told me, when I lived, because my art
To them seemed wide and spacious as the air,
That time would be pervaded everywhere
With it, until no work would have a part
That had not once awakened in my heart,
That everything would crooked be or fair
As it inherited its proper share
From me and could that share again impart.
But this strange present world is not of me.
If I could find somewhere a secret sign,
That one might say: In this an Ancient sings,
I should acknowledge then my legacy
And love to call this modern fabric mine.
Perhaps, once, in my sleep, I dreamed such things?

Angelica

Dirty bugger,
Swells around the corner
Never saw her.

Diamond in the rough,
Not a polished bluff,
But the real stuff.

Scuttling city elf,
Kept her tongue on the shelf,
Sang only to herself.

And her mother was a bum
And her father too drank some.
She was scum.

And her birth was unrecorded.
All the secrecy she hoarded
That an alley afforded.

Garbage was her rosary,
And flesh the martyry
Where garbage came out flowery.

What should she have been doing
Instead of brewing
Silver out of gutter-spewing?

Let her lurk
In the murk
Doing divine dirty work.

If God left her out of Creation,
Then God atoning in Damnation
Will find her Heaven and Salvation.

Or if he meant to leave her in,
Her blasphemy becomes His sin,
His purgatory all her vermin.

This is Angelica,
Singing through scrofula,
May she survive even Utopia.

Another Apple

Take care what piece of me you take to taste,
And prove me on no individual bite.
How many times your stupid mouth must waste
My fruit until it learns that even despite
My single rind no sample is the same
To eat and test me on, I shall but wait,
Fearing what hungry chance may yet inflame
The tooth's sharp appetite and drive it straight
Through this composite, non-committal meat
Into the secret and astringent core
Where bitter and entire this gall shall greet
The tongue's first touch. And you will need no more
To know me well and ever and thoroughly.
Short wit to who make their last meal of me.

Lady of All Creation

Lady of all creation and perverse,
Dressed as a drab, the sacrificial inverse
Of all the beauty of the universe:

Having to choose between the act and state,
Why should you rather labor and create
Than be the quiet unregenerate

Of being? Have you not a smile to show,
Who must creep out of sight and creep so low
That sight may be a heavenly thing to know?

We cannot find you in your fair device.
This place is like a godless paradise,
Fade as a wine unseasoned of a spice.

Appear! Be fair! and we who are the doing
Of your dark self-denial won't be ruing
The end of all our worlds beyond renewing,

If you rise from our ruin enchantedly
The loveliness you meant our share to be
And let us live in you invisibly.

Named

Dance it was and no one dancing,
Cool fire and full spirit,
Pure performing without pitying
Self of flaming feet,
Heart of heat.

Air imbibed it. It was air.
Yellow flushed when was sun.
No name bespoken, only fair
Played a light with light,
Both in fright.

Man on man went up to see,
Saying, woman must be here,
Such delight cannot be
Unlovable or needless of
Name and love.

Man on man went up to see.
Came but one woman down
Nighttime, breathing heavily
Love like a name in her,
Too dark to stir.

Summons

Come to me, man of my death –
Is it not death, what I am not,
The immanences not yet mine,
To be unbled with love?
I am a hollow without hunger.
Fate asks not to be fed but filled.
The end will be an end.
Stop up the narrow cyst
Most nothing when most provided.
The embrace imbibes us bodily.
Only the clasp and quiet stay
As death. Death must be something,
To have been made of us.

How impossible is abandoning;
Love is the lightest call,
But irresistable as death is.
The cruel internal I perceive
Under any mask. Beauty is a guise.
But destiny and the open flesh
Are more dire than beautiful.
I have a hound out that smells blood
In the whitest skin. I have a heart
Bleeding me hollow.
I can detect you as scent the dark,
With my eyes closed, truly.
Or, though my fingers turn in on me,
The thought of your thin face will be
Deep with the idea of your body.
Love is sure, life is more easily fled.
For life is only one in every one
And can escape itself without pursuit or heed.
Love is a place of numbers, where the conscience doubles.
It is the time, whenever it is the call.
Say no more it is not much,
No mystery unless we waste words on it,
Sob afterwards when we should be still,
Go on as ghosts when death is livelier,
Though strange, without a language,
And not unhappy, since there are no tongues.

21

To a Cautious Friend

Foresight may mask
As the prophetic faith only until
I need, I ask.
Then reason parts around you to fulfill
The friend I lose or win
As you go out, come in.

It never shall be I
Or anyone who heard the tale from me
To say which did you, why.
Love touched my eyes in time just not to see,
And better, before I begged a groat,
Love touched my throat.

Dallydilbaree

From the Fountain of Dallydilbaree
They had their loveliness, the ladies.
And modestly informed they were
Most intimately from afar, afar.
The source and spray were air before
The wind sipped and was consecrated
To blow around and around in pillaring whorls
Everywhere until everywhere girls
Grew delicately wisps and wreathings first
And flesh only as afterthought
And ladies next
And women last.

And as women bewailing
Beauty was a boon unbodily
Foamed windwise out of Dallydilbaree,
Fanned windwise back
After the interval of life
That is love in ladies.

The petulant prayers seeking the source,
The local breath betraying the essence
Large to the atmosphere again
And out of the air then into rain
Replenishing the far fountain,
Cannot spare the specific charms
Of Laura, Elinor or Kate
The incessant bubbling up of beauty
Gurgles and crowds to evaporate.

For ladies and love allow an end,
But the bottomless springs of Dallydilbaree
Are sunken through to the other side
Where ladies and liquids are compounded
Capriciously of nearly nothing
And sparkled up to quench and please
Men and other certainties
Unearthed here and hovering over
Dallydilbaree's brink. There many a lover
Sounding the evanescent silver

Thirsts his sad eyes down
The cavernous brown
Through to the blue
In which beauty must drown
Though bodies be buried.

Improprieties

I

Your hands are very white.
What fierceness have they fingered
To grow so delicate, so pale?
Are your feet whiter yet
And still more timorously slender
That they step so obscurely?
Are you afraid of hurting me
That you do not go barefooted?
But I am more aggrieved that two white shames
Should patter virtuously in sandals,
Demurely shod.

II

Why do you come indecorously bearing
Clusters of lilacs faceted elegantly?
They are an immorality to your chasteness.
For you are stark and inornate
And your hair is smooth and unfragrant
And your eyes are cold chalcedony
And your lips are a thin sharpness
And all the rest of you a dear severity.

III

Why do you come fantastically folded
In a reticent dark gown?
It is the house of a harlot
And you are white and unclothed inside.
Do you think you can dwell there
Cryptically forever
And yet be wantonly unviolated?

IV

But your gayest indecency
Is your garrulity
That lecherously enwraps your silence.
When will you be bared of your frivolity
And come to me mutely, modestly serious?

For One Who Will Dust a Shadow

Take out your speckled shadow
From its cupboard, in the morning.
Softly brush it,
Lest you crush it
And leave your body bare
With no shadow to wear.

And lift your little body
From its bed, in the morning.
When you've dressed it
And caressed it
In each careful counted way, then,
Put the speckled shadow on.

If at noon it may be found
Like a scarf upon your shoulder,
Be at dusk a little bolder,
Trail your shadow on the ground.

But at night, put away
Your shadow in its cupboard
That is empty all day
And upon its little bed
Lay your tired little body
Well washed and fed.

If you take these troubles
Exactly enough
To wear yourself out
In an accurate measure,
Then you and your body and your speckled shadow
Will all wear out quite evenly together
With nothing left over.

A Consolation

If I loved you yesterday,
Do not hope to-day or say:
We'll go traveling to-morrow
In the woods, perhaps to borrow
Silence from a thoughtful tree
To compose our jollity,
Taking love to be its student,
Making love more kind and prudent.

Do not hope – for yesterday
Was an old truth on the way
To an evening death and I
Can't be faithful to a lie.
I've another who perceives
Silence peering under leaves.
Do not hope, for my new truth
Has not memory or ruth.

Do not grieve, to-day will soon
Die upon the dying moon,
Leaving still a ghost behind
That may yet my love remind
Of an older love that died
And an honest truth denied,
Truth that yet came soon to die
And to haunt me with a lie.

Do not yet despair – to-morrow
May bring comfort to your sorrow.
It shall have another truth
That, in an ambitious youth
Seeking a new verity
To gain it eternity,
May, with wise and watchful eyes,
Find it in old loves and lies.

Summary for Alastor

Because my song was bold
And you knew but my song,
You thought it must belong
To one brave to behold.

But finding me a shy
And cool and quiet Eve,
You scarcely would believe
The fevered singer was I.

And you caressed the child
That blushed beneath your eyes,
Hoping you might surprise
The hidden heart and wild.

And being only human,
A proud, impetuous fool
Whose guise alone was cool,
I let you see the woman.

Yet, though I was beguiled
Through being all too human,
I'm glad you had the woman
And not the trustful child.

For though the woman's weeping
And still must weep awhile,
The dreaming child can smile
And keep on safely sleeping.

How I Called the Ant Darling

The moment must have been the same for both.
For, as my foot went down to kill it,
Darling, Darling, screamed it,
And Darling, Darling, I answered it,

Lifting on the crackling pieces,
And once more Darling as once more down.
Then it did not cry or turn.
My mouth stopped tasting Ant.

Death-making lost disgust,
Or death went from both, and it was
Darling, Darling, with no thought of pardon,
As if the dead and death-maker clasped hands,

Watching the thing.
So it was Darling, Darling,
Yet no peace, for I ached
As much as like Ant I could feel,

Not much: I could not crawl
Or break up so small.
My leg thought pain, but was too high
To see, except the humane toes

Drew in to hug the deed.
So Darling, in my mouth
Wore the sharp slaughter off.

The next breath, too, said Darling, but looking up
From murder with no purer word,
I breathed it no less tender
Not for an Ant and not for murder.

Forgotten Girlhood

Into Laddery Street

The stove was grey, the coal was gone.
In and out of the same room
One went, one came.
One turned into nothing.
One turned into whatever
Turns into children.

But remember the coal was gone.
Old Trouble carried her down
To her cellar where the rags were warm.

And turned her sooner
Than had her mother
Into one of the Laddery children,
And called her Lida
For short and for long,
For long, for long.

In Laddery Street

Herself

I am hands
And face
And feet
And things inside of me
That I can't see.

What knows in me?
Is it only something inside
That I can't see?

Children

Children sleep at night.
Children never wake up
When morning comes.
Only the old ones wake up.
Old Trouble is always awake.

31

Children can't see over their eyes.
Children can't hear beyond their ears.
Children can't know outside of their heads.

The old ones see.
The old ones hear.
The old ones know.
The old ones are old.

Toward the Corner

One, two, three.
Coming, Old Trouble, coming.
The organ-grinder is turning,
The children are sing-songing,
The organ-grinder is stopping,
The children are hum-coming,
Coming, Old Trouble, coming.

One, two, three.
Coming, Old Trouble, coming.
The bakeshop is sugar-crusting,
The children are window-tasting,
The bakeshop is shop-shutting,
The children are sugar-dreaming,
The children are sugar-stealing,
Coming, Old Trouble, coming.

One, two, three.
Coming, Old Trouble, coming.
Father Bell is evening-praying,
The night is empty-falling,
The rats are out,
The birds are in,
Coming, Old Trouble, coming.

One, two, three.
One, two, three.
Coming, Old Trouble, coming.
Somebody's dead, who can it be?
Old Trouble, is it you?

Then say so, say so.
One, two, three,
Into the great rag-bag you go.
Going, Old Trouble, going.

Around the Corner

But don't call Mother Damnable names.
The names will come back
At the end of a nine-tailed Damnable Strap.
Mother Damnable, Mother Damnable,
Good Mother Damnable.

Home, thieves, home.
Mother Damnable waits at her counting-table.
Thieves do the thieving,
But she does the counting.
Home, thieves, home.

Home Sparkey, home Dodo, home Henry, home Gring.
With Dodo I kiss,
With Henry and Gring
I go walking and talking,
With Sparkey I sing.

Then along comes Mother Damnable.
Off, thieves, off.
'Such nonsense is disgraceful among thieves.
Off, wench, off.'

A Second Away

One, two, three, four, more,
Knock at the door,
Come in, come in,
Stir the stew,
Warm love up
In a wooden pot
And serve it hot
With a wooden spoon.

Rap, rap,
Come in, come in,
Love's the only thing
That deceives enjoyably.
Mother Mary and her Magdalenes,
We don't care a curse how much we're deceived
Or deceive.

Hey, Lida,
Away, away,
On a hobby horse
That is wooden together
With everything else
But Lida, Lida.

Hey, hey,
Away, away,
Until Lida falls off
At any next turning.

At any next turning
Off may come falling
Lost lady with question-marks
All over her nose,
All over her nose.

All the Way Back

Bill Bubble in a bowler hat
Walking by picked Lida up.
Lida said 'I feel like dead.'
Bubble said
'Not dead but wed.'
No more trouble, no more trouble,
Safe in the arms of Husband Bubble.

A rocking chair, a velvet hat,
Greengrocer, dinner, a five-room flat,
Come in, come in,
Same old pot and wooden spoon,
But it's only soup staring up at the moon.

34

Have you heard about Bubble?
He was called away
To fight for his country
And got stuck in the chimney.
Then hey, Lida, away
On a hobby left over from Yesterday.

One, two, three,
Mother and Moon and Old Trouble and me.
How happy we'll be
Together and all raggedy.
I'm not a full yard,
Old Trouble's not a full inch,
The moon's a hole
And mother's a pinch.
The rest is tatters,
But to rag-pickers
Faults are perfection's faults,
And only perfection matters.

Incarnations

Do not deny,
Do not deny, thing out of thing.
Do not deny in the new vanity
The old, original dust.

From what grave, what past of flesh and bone
Dreaming, dreaming I lie
Under the fortunate curse,
Bewitched, alive, forgetting the first stuff...
Death does not give a moment to remember in

Lest, like a statue's too transmuted stone,
I grain by grain recall the original dust
And, looking down a stair of memory, keep saying:
This was never I.

Several Love-Stories

The formulas of recognition
Apply themselves to memories.
There's where,
There's when,
There's there.

Yes, a nice time.
I met three fishermen out on the bay
Who couldn't understand language.
I found a mercadon –
What's a mercadon? –
And dined with native nobility,
But there's no place like home!

Yes, true-love – not travel.
It was a sky
Not just to look at
But prove –
If possible,
If possible.

I went up of love,
I fell down of loves.
There's no place like home!

Townsfolk, untwirl these casings
From Paris and Heaven.

The Mask

Cover up,
Oh, quickly cover up
All the new spotted places,
All the unbeautifuls,
The insufficiently beloved.

With what? with what?
With the uncovering of the lovelies,
With the patches that transformed
The more previous corruptions.

Is there no pure then?
The eternal taint wears beauty like a mask.
But a mask eternal.

The Signature

The effort to put my essence in me
Ended in a look of beauty.
Such looks fanatically mean cruelness
Toward self; toward others, sweetness.

But ghostly is that essence
Of which I was religious.
Nor may I claim defeat
Since others find my look sweet
And marvel how triumphant
The mere experiment.

So I grow ghostly,
Though great sincerity
First held a glass up to my name.
And great sincerity claim
For beauty the live image,
But no deathly fame:
The clear face spells
A bright illegibility of name.

Chloe Or . . .

Chloe or her modern sister, Lil,
Stepping one day over the fatal sill,
Will say quietly: 'Behold the waiting equipage!'
Or whistle Hello and end an age.

For both these girls have that cold ease
Of women overwooed, half-won, hard to please.
Death is one more honour they accept
Quizzically, ladies adept

In hiding what they feel, if they feel at all.
It can scarcely have the importance of a ball,
Is less impressive than the least man
Chloe, smiling, turns pale, or Lil tweaks with her fan.

Yet, they have been used so tenderly.
But the embarrassment of the suit will be
Death's not theirs. They will avoid aggression
As usual, be saved by self-possession.

Both of them, or most likely, Lil,
No less immortal, will
Refuse to see anything distressing,
Keep Death, like all the others, guessing.

Yes and No

Across a continent imaginary
Because it cannot be discovered now
Upon this fully apprehended planet –
No more applicants considered,
Alas, alas –

Ran an animal unzoological,
Without a fate, without a fact,
Its private history intact
Against the travesty
Of an anatomy.

Not visible not invisible,
Removed by dayless night,
Did it ever fly its ground
Out of fancy into light,
Into space to replace
Its unwritable decease?

Ah, the minutes twinkle in and out
And in and out come and go
One by one, none by none,
What we know, what we don't know.

Chrysalis

Golden to itself it lay,
Its dreams as grains in twinkle-twinkle,
Inward only, to my eyes grey,
Mere cotton, mere butterfly to be.

The time of premonition is thought.
Long before flying, in my thought it flew,
On that day on a tree-side
An old butterfly was new,
Clung wet with fright to its wings.

I blew more fright upon it,
Helped it shudder dry.
Because it could not cry
Stuttering it flew among the vines.
Among the vines my own eyes failed.
'Come away,' they said,
'Out of sight is dead.'

So Slight

It was as near invisible
As night in early dusk.
So slight it was,
It was as unbelievable
As day in early dawn.

The summer impulse of a leaf
To flutter separately
Gets death and autumn.
Such faint rebellion
Was lately love in me.

So slight, it had no hope or sorrow,
It could but choose
A passing flurry for its nuptial,
Drift off and fall
Like thistledown without a bruise.

The Tillaquils

Dancing lamely on a lacquered plain,
Never a Tillaquil murmurs for legs.
Embrace rustles a windy wistfulness,
But feels for no hands.
Scant stir of being, yet rather they
Unfulfilled unborn than failing alive,
Escaping the public shame of history.

Once only two Tillaquils nearly a man and woman
Violated a hopeless code with hope,
Slept a single dream seeming in time.
'Come,' he cried, coaxing her,
'Stairs stream upward not for rest at every step
But to reach the top always before Death.'
'Softly,' she whispered,
'Or two Tillaquils will wake.'

Death they passed always over and over,
Life grew always sooner and sooner.
But love like a grimace
Too real on Life's face
Smiled two terrified dreams of Tillaquils
Tremblingly down the falling flights;
Who saved themselves in waking
The waste of being something
And danced traditionally
To nothingness and never;
With only a lost memory
Punishing this foolish pair
That nearly lived and loved
In one nightmare.

Take Hands

Take hands.
There is no love now.
But there are hands.
There is no joining now,
But a joining has been
Of the fastening of fingers
And their opening.
More than the clasp even, the kiss
Speaks loneliness,
How we dwell apart,
And how love triumphs in this.

Lucrece and Nara

Astonished stood Lucrece and Nara,
Face flat to face, one sense and smoothness.
'Love, is this face or flesh,
Love, is this you?'
One breath drew the dear lips close
And whispered,
'Nara, is there a miracle can last?'
'Lucrece, is there a simple thing can stay?'

Unnoticed as a single raindrop
Broke each dawn until
Blindness as the same day fell.
'How is the opalescence of my white hand, Nara?
Is it still pearly-cool?'
'How is the faintness of my neck, Lucrece?
Is it blood shy with warmth, as always?'

Ghostly they clung and questioned
A thousand years, not yet eternal,
True to their fading,
Through their long watch defying
Time to make them whole, to part them.

A gentle clasp and fragrance played and hung
A thousand years and more
Around earth closely.
'Earth will be long enough,
Love has no elsewhere.'

And when earth ended, was devoured
One shivering midsummer
At the dissolving border,
A sound of light was felt.
'Nara, is it you, the dark?'
'Lucrece, is it you, the quiet?'

The Sad Boy

Ay, his mother was a mad one
And his father was a bad one:
The two begot this sad one.

Alas for the single boot
The Sad Boy pulled out of the rank green pond,
Fishing for happiness
On the gloomy advice
Of a professional lover of small boys.

Pity the lucky Sad Boy
With but a single happy boot
And an extra foot
With no boot for it.

This was how the terrible hopping began
That wore the Sad Boy down
To a single foot
And started the great fright in the province
Where the Sad Boy became half of himself.

Wherever he went thumping and hopping,
Pounding a whole earth into a half-heaven,
Things split all around
Into a left side for the left magic,
Into no side for the missing right boot.

Mercy be to the Sad Boy,
Mercy be to the melancholy folk
On the Sad Boy's right.

It was not for clumsiness
He lost the left boot
And the knowledge of his left side,
But because one awful Sunday
This dear boy dislimbed
Went back to the old pond
To fish up the other boot
And was quickly (being too light for his line)
Fished in.

Gracious how he kicks now –
And the almost-ripples show
Where the Sad Boy went in
And his mad mother
And his bad father after him.

Mortal

There is a man of me that sows.
There is a woman of me that reaps.
One for good,
And one for fair,
And they cannot find me anywhere.

Father and Mother, shadowy ancestry,
Can you make no more than this of me?

The Quids

The little quids, the monstrous quids,
The everywhere, everything, always quids,
The atoms of the Monoton,
Each turned an essence where it stood,
Ground a gisty dust from its neighbours' edges,
Until a powdery thoughtfall stormed in and out –
The cerebration of a slippery quid enterprise.

Each quid stirred.
The united quids
Waved through a sinuous decision.
The quids, that had never done anything before
But be, be, be, be, be –
The quids resolved to predicate,
To dissipate themselves in grammar.

Oh, the Monoton didn't care,
For whatever they did –
The Monoton's contributing quids –
The Monoton would always remain the same.

A quid here and there gyrated in place-position,
While many turned inside-out for the fun of it.
And a few refused to be anything but
Simple unpredicated copulatives.
Little by little, this commotion of quids,
By ones, by tens, by casual millions,
Squirming within the state of things,
The metaphysical acrobats,
The naked, immaterial quids,
Turned in on themselves
And came out all dressed –
Each similar quid of the inward same,
Each similar quid dressed in a different way,
The quids' idea of a holiday.

The quids could never tell what was happening.
But the Monoton felt itself differently the same
In its different parts.

The silly quids upon their learned exercise
Never knew, could never tell
What their wisdom was about,
What their carnival was like,
Being in, being in, being always in
Where they never could get out
Of the everywhere, everything, always in,
To derive themselves from the Monoton.

Afternoon

The fever of afternoon
Is called afternoon,
Old sleep uptorn,
Not yet time for night-time,
No other name, for no names
In the afternoon but afternoon.

Love tries to speak but sounds
So close in its own ear.
The clock-ticks hear
The clock-ticks ticking back.
The fever fills where throats show,
But nothing in these horrors moves to swallow
While thirst trails afternoon
To husky sunset.

Evening appears with mouths
When afternoon can talk.
Supper and bed open and close
And love makes thinking dark.
More afternoons divide the night,
New sleep uptorn,
Wakeful suspension between dream and dream –
We never knew how long.
The sun is late by hours of soon and soon –
Then comes the quick fever, called day.
But the slow fever is called afternoon.

No More Are Lovely Palaces

No more are lovely palaces
And Taj-Mahal is old.
The listening tenements,
The wakeful entertainments,
Waited wide and many ages
For the spirits of the promises
That more than men would come,
Would come the visitants evoked
By lovely palaces
And such emblazoned places
Men would never light for men.

A little surer now you know
They do not come the way you go.
And better build you and more soberly –
Houses fitter for you to leave
Than to receive
The more than haughty hosts
Of the imperishable ghosts,
That swing death's doors
And suck you into topless palaces,
Untrembling on the blowing bluish spaces,
Where you gasp out your gratitude
And say breathless:
Heaven's hand is not gentle,
The lovely palaces were too lovely,
True lavish is the terrible.

Goat and Amalthea

I have been assaulted by the moths
Thick in my eyes and throat many a night
When the thought of Amalthea was
Tall flame in the grimy wick.
Then I have blown the light out
And not remembered.
It is better to be dark with Amalthea
Than give her over to the moths and bats.

And Amalthea does not marvel that I can laugh
Or open my eyes to other eyes so brightly
Or strum upon my tongue
My best ballads over so merrily.

She fell of no plague or passion.
She was only swift, so swift, they say,
She ran till she stood still
As a bell swung round more than rings,
And was alive and dead in one day.
When the day went she was dead most fully.
She knew all.

I have come with Amalthea in my veins
Into a fifth season. Time is more than slow.
For winter is over, yet I see no summer.
Now it is always snow.

But I am love of her and I am now.
And she is death of me and she was long ago.
The centuries I weep her bring us nearer.
Yet we can never touch.
For Amalthea in her former time
Shall weep me longer.

The Virgin

My flesh is at a distance from me.
Yet approach and touch it:
It is as near as anyone can come.

This vestiary stuff
Is a true relic,
Though I have never worn it,
Though I shall never be dead.

And the possession?
The violence will be over,
A forgotten passion,
Before I learn of it.

To a Loveless Lover

1.
How we happened to be both human,
Of the material of the machine...

The one original substance is one.
Two is two's destruction.
But love is the single word wherein
The double murder of the machine
Is denied
In one suicide...

Long very long ago,
A time unthinkable,
We loved each other.

Greet an old doubt
With contemporary conviction –
Lest going you give me lovelessness
And the accursed courage for a close.

2.
Did I surprise too truly, then,
Your all too prompt anticipation,
Tear down the wall of self,
Expose the terror of fulfilment?

As from a balcony,
Applaud the way I build the wall again.

3.
The requisite spot of anguish having shown
Upon my cheek the growth of the disease
From the internal infection of the bone
To the full epidermal fever, please
Proceed as you intended, in the tone
With which your parting sonnet tried to freeze
My too unliterary passion to stone.

Though love is not yet dead, your lyric crow,
Smelling the near-corruption, may come and perch
In antecedent mourning, not to sing
But consecrate to your pedantic church
His ultra-polite yet energetic wing
That flaps your piety incognito.

4.
The cycle of revenge comes round,
Your expiation ties in me.

Mercy, mercy for me
Who would only suffer,
Who would never sin.
The righteous are transfixed
While sinners are swept round to judgement.
Mercy, mercy for me where I stand
A bigot of forgiveness.

Druida

Above Druida, below Druida,
Round Druida when she loved,
The air and earth,
The grass and clouds,
Were golden, were laden,
Not with love – oh, less ethereal
Her radiation –
But with him heavily.

Her trance of him was timeless.
Her space of him was edgeless.
But meagre was the man,
He took ambition.
He heard a clock,
He saw a road.
When the clock struck,
Where the road began,
He called farewell to Druida.

A hundred huts heard the cry.
The heavy earth, the heavy air,
Lightened, melted.
The man was gone.
Druida laughed.
Follow him, follow him,
A hundred sisters said.

Druida followed.
Not to bless him, not to curse him,
Not to bring back the bridegroom,
But to pass him like a blind bird
Seeing all heaven ahead.

She follows him, she follows him,
A hundred sisters said,
Standing at their doors while the man fled
And Druida smiled along.

Druida found the sky.
Earth was but imagination,
Love but self-alienation,
Man but a lover not love.

She has passed him, she has passed him,
A hundred sisters cried.
And the man turned back.
And a hundred passions welcomed him
In a hundred huts.

Back to the Mother Breast

Back to the mother breast
In another place –
Not for milk, not for rest,
But the embrace
Clean bone
Can give alone.

The cushioning years
Afraid of closer kiss
Put cure of tears
Before analysis;
And the vague infant cheek
Turned away to speak.

Now back to the mother breast,
The later lullaby exploring,
The deep bequest
And franker singing
Out of the part
Where there is no heart.

As Well as Any Other

As well as any other, Erato,
I can dwell separately on what we know
In common secrecy,
And celebrate the old, adoréd rose,
Retell – oh why – how similarly grows
The last leaf of the tree.

But for familiar sense what need can be
Of my most singular device or me,
If homage may be done
(Unless it is agreed we shall not break
The patent silence for mere singing's sake)
As well by anyone?

Mistrust me not, then, if I have begun
Unwontedly and if I seem to shun
Unstrange and much-told ground:
For in peculiar earth alone can I
Construe the word and let the meaning lie
That rarely may be found.

John and I

Begin the story with a man; curtail
The matter of his hair and hands and eyes.
The simple character will be enough
For bearing out the name – pass by the flesh,
Since this is but a tale and therefore clean
Of the decay that dresses up the soul.
Then tell the wife and woman at one stroke
And let the detail lie uncut upon
The monument of this small artifice.
There was a man to be delivered of
His wife as of a poor witch of the shades
Of plausibility. The unasked help
Of that old fury, accident, sufficed.
She died or was devoured in one swift night
She ripped apart and sewed herself into,
A weighted sack that never bubbled once,
And sank. Perceive him madder than before,
With nothing but a nasty vacancy
In the dark, gangrened spot upon his brain
That she had occupied – repudiation,
But nothing more: an itching, empty sore
That better had been left incurable.
The uselessness of words about this case
Is obvious. The literary end
Establishes a certain calm in us,
If not in him; and he may stop, fall out,
For all we know or care, where we leave off.
And yet, if this is death, how listlessly,
How indecisively, the sentence drops,
And not through pity but embarrassment,
The provocation seeming trivial.

Then strip the narrative of mystery
And let it shiver out the meaning like
A naked foetus parted from its womb:
This way a character becomes a man
Impossible to end in words or their
Equivalent in silence. Therefore find
The fellow a good name. John makes a frame
That any not too fanciful idea

Or man can fit into.... And John looked out,
Deduced his world and wisdom from the sins
And freaks of creatures not designedly
Alive, but born just in the course of things;
Construed his house among the others....

He was a man as far as he could see,
And where he could not, I, his chronicler,
Began. The woman, among other things,
Confused the issue – yet it was as bad
After her going, for there seems to be
Nothing for me to talk about. A touch
Of night falls upon both of us. John sleeps,
Or else I sleep, my words obscure my words.
I have not done and yet I can't go on –
The articles that make us two divide us,
I am aware only of certain rules
By which he's rhetoric and I a fool,
The one who sets the problem, frets and loves,
While John evades, equivocates, evades.

There was an insufficiency in me
To which no one but John could minister,
A hunger no mere man could satisfy.
If I infringed upon the laws of art
By making John outlast himself till now,
It was to save him from the consequence
Of his genetic artfulness and falseness –
Defection, malice and oblivion.
The laws of art? Could I not alter them?
The reason I must call the passion dead
Lies in an insufficiency in him
That leaves me stranded in a half-told tale.
His name is cold. Life feels the loss when death
Takes off a man, and not at all the corpse;
And so with John and me. Nor do I weep
Or yet deny, confronted with the shame
Of a but literary authorship,
That John and I are better off like this.

Lying Spying

(Lying spying what men say of dead men,
What men say of me –
I can't remember anything.
Why can't I remember
What I alive knew of death
I dead know nothing of?)

'Poor John, John, John, John, John,'
Said the parson as he perched
On the sharp left discomfort
Of John John's tombstone –
John, John, John, John, John.

Cobbler on the right
Hammered out the memory
Of the nails of John's soles.
Mercer in the middle
Remembered the measure
Of John's extraordinary shroud.

But no further the parson, the cobbler, the mercer,
Lying spying
In the graveyard,
Where night fell deeper darker,
Dead men mumbled, might be mumbling,
Something secret about life.

Lying spying
John, John, John, John, John,
Parson, cobbler, mercer, parson.

The Lullaby

Every poor fellow reminds me of my father.
With worse luck than that
He reminds me of my father
With worse luck than he had.
Which means me
Who have better luck than my father had
Because it is worse than bad.

Every fine fellow reminds me of me.
Good luck is hard come by.
It is not that innocency
Of how luck befalls.
It is a bad luck weary,
A worse luck turned into destiny,
A knowledge of bad luck
And with bad luck seamy.

A poor fellow knows a poor fellow.
A fine fellow knows a poor fellow and a fine fellow,
A poor fellow and a poor fellow.
Every poor fellow reminds me of me.
Every fine fellow reminds me of my father.

And it is not to be forgotten:
All luck is luck,
My father's or mine.
He was a poor fellow.
His bad luck was perhaps no luck.
I am a fine fellow.
My good luck is perhaps no luck.
All luck is perhaps no luck.
All luck is luck or perhaps no luck.

For is this a way to divide,
By poorness and fineness,
By pity and pride?
Comparison of luck is how
All babies cry.
Mother! Cease rocking, promising,

Let us all choke
Rather than sob asleep
With pout of luck on every lip
Resentful birth renewing.

Helen's Burning

Her beauty, which we talk of,
Is but half her fate.
All does not come to light
Until the two halves meet
And we are silent
And she speaks,
Her whole fate saying,
She is, she is not, in one breath.

But we tell only half, fear to know all
Lest all should be to tell
And our mouths choke with flame
Of her consuming
And lose the gift of prophecy.

Helen's Faces

Bitterly have I been contested for,
Though never have I counted numbers –
They were too many, less than all.
And kindly have I warded off
Contest and bitterness,
Given each a replica of love,
Beguiled them with fine images.

To their hearts they held them.
Her dear face, its explicitness!
Clearly, of all women, the immediate one
To these immediate men.

But the original woman is mythical,
Lies lonely against no heart.
Her eyes are cold, see love far off,
Read no desertion when love removes,
The images out of fashion.

Undreamed of in her many faces
That each kept off the plunderer:
Contest and bitterness never raged round her.

The Tiger

The tiger in me I know late, not burning bright.
Of such women as I am, they say,
'Woman, many women in one,' winking.
Such women as I say, thinking,
'A procession of one, reiteration
Of blinking eyes and disentangled brains
Measuring their length in love.
Each yard of thought is an embrace.
To these I have charms.
Shame, century creature.'
To myself, hurrying, I whisper,
'The lechery of time greases their eyes.
Lust, earlier than time,
Unwinds their minds.
The green anatomy of desire
Plain as through glass
Quickens as I pass.'

Earlier than lust, not plain,
Behind a darkened face of memory,
My inner animal revives.
Beware, that I am tame.
Beware philosophies
Wherein I yield.

They cage me on three sides.
The fourth is glass.
Not to be image of the beast in me,
I press the tiger forward.
I crash through.
Now we are two.
One rides.

And now I know the tiger late,
And now they pursue:
'A woman in a skin, mad at her heels
With pride, pretending chariot wheels –
Fleeing our learned days,
She reassumes the brute.'

The first of the pursuers found me.
With lady-ears I listened.
'Dear face, to find you here
After such tiger-hunt and pressing of
Thick forest, to find you here
In high house in a jungle,
To brave as any room
The tiger-cave and as in any room
Find woman in the room
With dear face shaking her dress
To wave like any picture queen...'
'Dear pursuer, to find me thus
Belies no tiger. The tiger runs and rides,
But the lady is not venturous.
Like any picture queen she hides
And is unhappy in her room,
Covering her eyes against the latest year,
Its learning of old queens,
Its death to queens and pictures,
Its lust of century creatures,
And century creatures as one woman,
Such a woman as I,
Mirage of all green forests –
The colour of the season always
When hope lives of abolished pleasures.'

So to the first pursuer I prolonged
Woman's histories and shames,
And yielded as became a queen
Picture-dreaming in a room
Among silk provinces where pain
Ruined her body without stain –
So white, so out of time, so story-like.
While woman's pride escaped
In tiger stripes.

Hymn to the hostage queen
And her debauched provinces.
Down fell her room,
Down fell her high couches.
The first pursuer rose from his hot cloak.

'Company,' he cried, 'the tiger made magic
While you slept and I dreamt of ravages.
The queen was dust.'
And Queen, Queen, Queen,
Crowded the Captain's brain.
And Queen, Queen, Queen,
Spurred the whole train
With book-thoughts
And exploits of queen's armies
On gold and silver cloth.
Until they stumbled on their eyes,
Read the number of the year,
Remembered the fast tiger.

The tiger recalled man's fear
Of beast, in man-sweat they ran back,
Opened their books at the correct pages.
The chapter closed with queens and shepherdesses.
'Peace to their dim tresses,'
Chanted the pious sages.

And now the tiger in me I knew late.
'O pride,' I comforted, 'rest.
The mischief and the rape
Cannot come through.
We are in the time of never yet
Where bells peal backward,
Peal "forget, forget".'

Here am I found forgotten.
The sun is used. The men are in the book.
I, woman, have removed the window
And read in my high house in the dark,
Sitting long after reading, as before,
Waiting, as in the book, to hear the bell,
Though long since has fallen away the door,
Long since, when like a tiger I was pursued
And the first pursuer, at such and such a date,
Found how the tiger takes the lady
Far away where she is gentle.
In the high forest she is gentle.

She is patient in a high house.
Ah me, ah me, says every lady in the end,
Putting the tiger in its cage
Inside her lofty head.
And weeps reading her own story.
And scarcely knows she weeps,
So loud the tiger roars.
Or thinks to close her eyes,
Though surely she must be sleeping,
To go on without knowing weeping,
Sleeping or not knowing,
Not knowing weeping,
Not knowing sleeping.

The Rugged Black of Anger

The rugged black of anger
Has an uncertain smile-border.
The transition from one kind to another
May be love between neighbour and neighbour;
Or natural death; or discontinuance
Because, so small is space,
The extent of kind must be expressed otherwise;
Or loss of kind when proof of no uniqueness
Confutes the broadening edge and discourages.

Therefore and therefore all things have experience
Of ending and of meeting,
And of ending that much more
As self grows faint of self dissolving
When more is the intenser self
That is another too, or nothing.
And therefore smiles come of least smiling –
The gift of nature to necessity
When relenting grows involuntary.

This is the account of peace,
Why the rugged black of anger
Has an uncertain smile-border,
Why crashing glass does not announce
The monstrous petal-advance of flowers,
Why singleness of heart endures
The mind coupled with other creatures.
Room for no more than love in such dim passages
Where between kinds lie only
Their own uncertain edges.

This such precise division of space
Leaves nothing for walls, nothing but
Weakening of place, gentleness.
The blacker anger, blacker the less
As anger greater, angrier grows;
And least where most,
Where anger and anger meet as two
And share one smile-border
To remain so.

Echoes

1.

Since learning all in such a tremble last night –
Not with my eyes adroit in the dark,
But with my fingers hard with fright,
Astretch to touch a phantom, closing on myself –
I have been smiling.

2.

Mothering innocents to monsters is
Not of fertility but fascination
In women.

3.

It was the beginning of time
When selfhood first stood up in the slime.
It was the beginning of pain
When an angel spoke and was quiet again.

4.

After the count of centuries numbers hang
Heavy over the unnumbered hopes and oppress
The heart each woman stills beneath her dress
Close to the throat, where memory clasps the lace,
An ancient brooch.

5.

It is a mission for men to scare and fly
After the siren luminary, day.
Someone must bide, someone must guard the night.

6.

If there are heroes anywhere
Unarm them quickly and give them
Medals and fine burials
And history to look back on
As weathermen point with pride to rain.

7.

Dire necessity made all,
Made the most frightful first,
Then less and less dire the need
Until in that world horrors were least
And haunting meant never to see ghosts.

8.

Intelligence in ladies and gentlemen
And their children
Draws a broad square of knowledge
With their house walls.
But four corners to contain a square
Yield to an utmost circle –
The garden of the perpendicular is a sphere.

9.

Need for a tragic head,
Though no occasion now to grieve,
In that mere mental time
When tears are thought of and none appear.

10.

The optician, in honour of his trade,
Wore the most perfect spectacles ever made,
Saw his unspectacled mother and father
And all his unspectacled relatives with anger,
On holidays for spite never went home
But put away his spectacles to visit Rome,
And indulged his inherited astigmatism
As the vacation privilege of an optician,
Squinting up at the Cathedral
As the Romans thought cultivated and natural.

11.

'I shall mend it,' I say,
Whenever something breaks,
'By tying the beginning to the end.'
Then with my hands washed clean

And fingers piano-playing
And arms bare to go elbow-in,
I come to an empty table always.
The broken pieces do not wait
On rolling up of sleeves.
I come in late always
Saying, 'I shall mend it.'

12.
Gently down the incline of the mind
Speeds the flower, the leaf, the time –
All but the fierce name of the plant,
Imperishable matronymic of a species.

13.
The poppy edifices of sleep,
The monotonous musings of night-breath,
The liquid featureless interior faces,
The shallow terrors, waking never far.

14.
Love at a sickbed is a long way
And an untastable thing.
It hangs like a sickroom picture
And wears like another's ring.
Then the guarded yawn of pain snaps,
The immeasurable areas of distress
. . . . . . collapse . . .

15.
. . . cheated history –
Which stealing now has only then
And stealing us has only them.

16.
Now victory has come of age,
Learned in arts of desolation,

Gifted with death, love of decline,
Hunger of waste and fresh corruption.
And here it softens and laments,
Mourns fallen enemies, kisses the razed cities,
Hovers where sense has been,
In a ravished world, and calls the pities.

17.
Forgive me, giver, if I destroy the gift!
It is so nearly what would please me,
I cannot but perfect it.

18.
'Worthy of a jewel,' they say of beauty,
Uncertain what is beauty
And what the precious thing.

19.
And if occasionally a rhyme appeared,
This was the illness but not the death
So fear-awaited that hope of it
Ailing forgetfulness became.

20.
In short despite of time, that long despite of truth
By all that's false and would be true as true,
Here's truth in time, and false as false,
To say, 'Let truth be so-and-so
In ways so opposite, there's no
Long-short of it to reason more.'

21.
Between the word and the world lie
Fading eternities of soon.

22.

When a dog lying on the flagstones
Gazes into the sea of spring,
The surface of instruction
Does not ripple once:
He watches it too well.

23.

Love is very everything, like fire:
Many things burning,
But only one combustion.

24.

My address? At the cafés, cathedrals,
Green fields, marble terminals –
I teem with place.
When? Any moment finds me,
Reiterated morsel
Expanded into space.

25.

Let us seem to speak
Or they will think us dead, revive us.
Nod brightly, Hour.
Rescue us from rescue.

26.

What a tattle-tattle we.
And what a rattle-tattle me.
What a rattle-tattle-tattle-rattle we-me.
What a rattle-tattle.
What a tattle-rattle.
What a we.
What a me.
What a what a
What a
What

An Ageless Brow

This resolve: with trouble's brow
To forswear trouble and keep
A surface innocence and sleep
To smooth the mirror
With never, never,
And now, now.

The image, not yet in recognition, had grace
To be lasting in death's time, to postpone the face
Until the face had gone.
Her regiments sprang up here and fell of peace,
Her banners dropped like birds that had never flown.

And her arrested hand, clasping its open palm,
Pressed on from finger to finger
The stroke withheld from trouble
Till it be only ageless brow,
A renunciatory double
Of itself, a resolve of calm,
Of never, never, and now, now.

There is Much at Work

There is much at work to make the world
Surer by being more beautiful.
But too many beauties overwhelm the proof.
Too much beauty is Lethe.

The succession of fair things
Delights, does not enlighten.
We still know nothing, nothing.
Beauty will be truth but once.

Exchange the multiplied bewilderment
For a single presentation of fact by fairness;
And the revelation will be instantaneous.
We shall all die quickly.

Many Gentlemen

Many gentlemen there are born not babes.
They will be babes, they will be babes
In the shades.
They will dribble, they will babble,
They will pule in pantomime
Who were not babes in baby time.

Of such infant sorrow
Will they whimper
On Diotima's bosom
In the shades to-morrow:
Many gentlemen, many gentlemen frowning,
But not Socrates simpering among these,
Who was well weaned of her honey
In his prime and needs no pap now,
Having then long with baby eyes
Smiled upward to her learned brow.

The Map of Places

The map of places passes.
The reality of paper tears.
Land and water where they are
Are only where they were
When words read *here* and *here*
Before ships happened there.

Now on naked names feet stand,
No geographies in the hand,
And paper reads anciently,
And ships at sea
Turn round and round.
All is known, all is found.
Death meets itself everywhere.
Holes in maps look through to nowhere.

Death as Death

To conceive death as death
Is difficulty come by easily,
A blankness fallen among
Images of understanding,
Death like a quick cold hand
On the hot slow head of suicide.
So is it come by easily
For one instant. Then again furnaces
Roar in the ears, then again hell revolves,
And the elastic eye holds paradise
At visible length from blindness,
And dazedly the body echoes
'Like this, like this, like nothing else.'

Like nothing – a similarity
Without resemblance. The prophetic eye,
Closing upon difficulty,
Opens upon comparison,
Halving the actuality
As a gift too plain, for which
Gratitude has no language,
Foresight no vision.

The Troubles of a Book

The trouble of a book is first to be
No thoughts to nobody,
Then to lie as long unwritten
As it will lie unread,
Then to build word for word an author
And occupy his head
Until the head declares vacancy
To make full publication
Of running empty.

The trouble of a book is secondly
To keep awake and ready
And listening like an innkeeper,
Wishing, not wishing for a guest,
Torn between hope of no rest
And hope of rest.
Uncertainly the pages doze
And blink open to passing fingers
With landlord smile, then close.

The trouble of a book is thirdly
To speak its sermon, then look the other way,
Arouse commotion in the margin,
Where tongue meets the eye,
But claim no experience of panic,
No complicity in the outcry.
The ordeal of a book is to give no hint
Of ordeal, to be flat and witless
Of the upright sense of print.

The trouble of a book is chiefly
To be nothing but book outwardly;
To wear binding like binding,
Bury itself in book-death,
Yet to feel all but book;
To breathe live words, yet with the breath
Of letters; to address liveliness
In reading eyes, be answered with
Letters and bookishness.

The Wind Suffers

The wind suffers of blowing,
The sea suffers of water,
And fire suffers of burning,
And I of a living name.

As stone suffers of stoniness,
As light of its shiningness,
As birds of their wingedness,
So I of my whoness.

And what the cure of all this?
What the not and not suffering?
What the better and later of this?
What the more me of me?

How for the pain-world to be
More world and no pain?
How for the old rain to fall
More wet and more dry?

How for the wilful blood to run
More salt-red and sweet-white?
And how for me in my actualness
To more shriek and more smile?

By no other miracles,
By the same knowing poison,
By an improved anguish,
By my further dying.

Ding-Donging

With old hours all belfry heads
Are filled, as with thoughts.
With old hours ring the new hours
Between their bells.
And this hour-long ding-donging
So much employs the hour-long silences
That bells hang thinking when not striking,
When striking think of nothing.

Chimes of forgotten hours
More and more are played
While bells stare into space,
And more and more space wears
A look of having heard
But hearing not:
Forgotten hours chime louder
In the meantime, as if always,
And spread ding-donging back
More and more to yesterdays.

You or You

How well, you, you resemble!
Yes, you resemble well enough yourself
For me to swear the likeness
Is no other and remarkable
And matchless and so that
I love you therefore.

And all else which is very like,
Perfect counterfeit, pure almost,
Love, high animation, loyal unsameness –
To the end true, unto
Unmasking, self.

I am for you both sharp and dull.
I doubt thoroughly
And thoroughly believe.
I love you doubly,
How well, you, you deceive,
How well, you, you resemble.
I love you therefore.

Grace

This posture and this manner suit
Not that I have an ease in them
But that I have a horror
And so stand well upright –
Lest, should I sit and, flesh-conversing, eat,
I choke upon a piece of my own tongue-meat.

All Nothing, Nothing

The standing-stillness,
The from foot-to-foot,
Is no real illness,
Is no true fever,
Is no deep shiver;
The slow impatience
Is no sly conscience;
The covered cough bodes nothing,
Nor the covered laugh,
Nor the eye-to-eye shifting
Of the foot-to-foot lifting,
Nor the hands under-over,
Nor the neck and the waist
Twisting loose and then tight,
Right, left and right,
Nor the mind up and down
The long body column
With a know-not-why passion
And a can't-stop motion:
All nothing, nothing.

More death and discomfort
Were it
To walk away.
To fret and fidget
Is the ordinary.
To writhe and wriggle
Is the usual;
To walk away
Were a disgrace,
Were cowardice,
Were malice,
Would leave a mark and space
And were unbeautiful
And vain, oh, it were vain,
For none may walk away –
Who go, they stay,
And this is plain
In being general.

What, is their suspense
Clownish pretence?
What, are their grimaces
Silly-faces
And love of ghastliness?
What, is their anxiety and want
Teasing and taunt?
This scarcely,
This were a troublesome
Hypocrisy.

No, the twisting does not turn,
The stamping does not steam,
Nor the impatience burn,
Nor the tossing hearts scream,
Nor the bones fall apart
By the tossing of the heart,
Nor the heads roll off
With laugh-cough, laugh-cough,
Nor the backs crack with terror,
Nor the faces make martyr,
Nor love loathe
Nor loathing fondle
Nor pain rebel
Nor pride quarrel
Nor anything stir
In this stirring and standstill
Which is not natural,
Which is not trivial,
Not peaceful, not beautiful,
Altogether unwoeful,
Without significance
Or indeed further sense
Than going and returning
Within one inch,
Than rising and falling
Within one breath,
Than sweltering and shivering
Between one minute and the next
In the most artless
And least purposeful
Possible purpose.

Sea, False Philosophy

Foremost of false philosophies,
The sea harangues the daft,
The possessed logicians of romance.
Their swaying gaze, that swaying mass
Embrace in everlasting loss –
Sea is the spurned dust
Sifted with fine renunciation
Into a metaphor,
A slow dilution.

The drifting rhythms mesmerize
The speechless book of dreams.
The lines intone but are not audible.
The course is overtrue and knows
Neither a wreckage nor a sequel.

Optimisms in despair
Embark upon this apathetic frenzy.
Brains baffled in their eyes
Rest on this picture of monotony
And swoon with thanks.
Ah, hearts whole so peculiarly,
Heaven keep you by such argument
Persuaded and unbroken,
Heaven keep you if it can
As visions widen to a watery zero
And prophecy expands into extinction.

World's End

The tympanum is worn thin.
The iris is become transparent.
The sense has overlasted.
Sense itself is transparent.
Speed has caught up with speed.
Earth rounds out earth.
The mind puts the mind by.
Clear spectacle: where is the eye?

All is lost, no danger
Forces the heroic hand.
No bodies in bodies stand
Oppositely. The complete world
Is likeness in every corner.
The names of contrast fall
Into the widening centre.
A dry sea extends the universal.

No suit and no denial
Disturb the general proof.
Logic has logic, they remain
Locked in each other's arms,
Or were otherwise insane,
With all lost and nothing to prove
That even nothing can live through love.

Rhythms of Love

1.

Woman, reviling term
Of Man unto the female germ,
And Man, reproach of Woman
In this colloquy,
Have grown so contrary
That to have love
We must combine chastely next
Among the languages
Where calling is obscene
And words no more than mean.

2.

'Yes!' to you is in the same breath
'No! No!' to Death.
And your 'Yes! Yes!' to me
Is 'No!' to Death once angrily.
The Universe, leaning from a balcony,
Says: 'Death comes home to me
Covered with glory, when with such love.'
But such love turns into another stair.
Death and the Universe are an earlier pair.

3.

Dark image of my mind,
Shadow of my heart,
Second footfall and third
Partner of my doubleness
And fourth of this –
Love stops me short of counting to the end
Where numbers fail and fall to two,
Then one, then nothing, then you.

4.

Our months astonish, as meals come round.
So late! so soon!
We cry waterily like a pair of pigeons
Exclaiming whenever nothing happens
But commotion inwardly irises their bosoms.
And little more we know.
Our mouths open wide, our breath comes quick,
We gape like the first ones
And look to magic.

5.

In these embraces glamour
Comes early and is an early go-er.
After we have fictitiousness
Of our excess
All will be as before.
We shall say: Love is no more
Than waking, smiling,
Forcing out 'good morning',
And were it more it were
Fictitiousness and loving.

6.

You bring me messages
From days and years
In your time-clouded eyes
And I reply to these
And we know nothing of each other
But a habit, and this is ancient.
How we approach is hidden in a dream.
We close our eyes, we clutch at bodies,
We rise at dream's length from each other
And love mysteriously and coldly
Strangers we seem to love by memory.

7.

A brick and mortar motley,
A heart and mind confusion,
Built this Academy
And this Instruction.
We wag to bells
And wear the cap too high,
The gothic Axiom of Joy.
We know which jingling spells
Which understanding, but jingling
Is all our understanding.
Like dunces we still shall kiss
When graduated from love-making.

Dear Possible

Dear possible, and if you drown,
Nothing is lost, unless my empty hands
Claim the conjectured corpse
Of empty water – a legal vengeance
On my own earnestness.

Dear creature of event, and if I wait the clock,
And if the clock be punctual and you late,
Rail against me, my time, my clock,
And rightfully correct me
With wrong, lateness and ill-temper.

Dear scholar of love,
If by your own formula
I open heaven to you
When you knock punctually at the door,
Then you are there, but I where I was.

And I mean that fate in the scales
Is up, down, even, trembling,
Right, wrong, weighing and unweighing,
And I mean that, dear possible,
That fate, that dear fate.

O Vocables of Love

O vocables of love,
O zones of dreamt responses
Where wing on wing folds in
The negro centuries of sleep
And the thick lips compress
Compendiums of silence –

Throats claw the mirror of blind triumph,
Eyes pursue sight into the heart of terror.
Call within call
Succumbs to the indistinguishable
Wall within wall
Embracing the last crushed vocable,
The spoken unity of efforts.

O vocables of love,
The end of an end is an echo,
A last cry follows a last cry.
Finality of finality
Is perfection's touch of folly.
Ruin unfolds from ruin.
A remnant breeds a universe of fragment.
Horizons spread intelligibility
And once more it is yesterday.

In Nineteen Twenty-Seven

1.

In nineteen twenty-seven, in the spring
And opening summer, dull imagination
Stretched the dollish smile of people.
Behind plate-glass the slant deceptive
Of footwear and bright foreign affairs
Dispelled from consciousness those bunions
By which feet limp and nations farce –
O crippled government of leather –
And for a season (night-flies dust the evening)
Deformed necessity had a greening.

Then, where was I, of this time and my own
A double ripeness and perplexity?
Fresh year of time, desire,
Late year of my age, renunciation –
Ill-mated pair, debating if the window
Is worth leaping out of, and by whom.

If this is ghostly?
And in what living knowledge
Do the dressed skeletons walk upright?
They memorize their doings and lace the year
Into their shoes each morning,
Groping their faulty way,
These citizens of habit, by green and pink
In gardens and smiles in shops and offices;
Are no more real than this.

2.

And they are vast preliminaries:
Cohorts of hours marching upon the one
That must reduce and tell them.
Much must pass to be much vain –
Many minor and happy themes
For one unhappy major dissolution.

The calendar and clock have stopped,
But does the year run down in time?
While time goes round? Giddying
With new renewal at each turning?

Thus sooner than it knows narrows
A year a year a year to another.
The season loses count, speeds on.
But I, charmed body of myself,
Am struck with certainty, stop in the street,
Cry 'Now' – and in despair seize love,
A short despair, soon over.
For by now all is history.

Do we not live? We live. And love? We love.
But I? But you? We are but we.
A long table lies between us
Of talk and wood.
The best is to go out.
'Unpleasant weather,' banks and bakers say,
'But fine weather promised for to-morrow.'
To-morrow is when? This question
Turns heaviness of hours into affection:
Home for a place to lean an elbow.

3.

Fierce is unhappiness, a living god
Of impeccable cleanliness and costume.
In his intense name I wear
A brighter colour for the year
And with sharp step I praise him
That unteaches ecstasy and fear.
If I am found eating, loving,
Pleasure-making with the citizens,
These are the vigours learned of newspapers:
By such formalities I inhale
The corrupt oxygen of time
And reconstruct a past in which to wait
While the false curve of motion twitches straight.

Love me not less, next to myself
Most unloyal of the citizens,
That I thus worship with
The hourly population.
For by such looseness
I argue you with my tight conscience
And take you for so long, an empty term,
An irony of dearness.
And this is both love and not love,
And what I pledge both true and not true,
Since I am moved to speak by the season,
Bold and shy speed and recession,
Climax and suspension.

4.
Had I remained hidden and unmoved,
Who would have carried on this conversation
And at the close remembered the required toast
To the new year and the new deaths?
Oh, let me be choked ceremoniously
With breath and language, if I will,
And make a seemly world of it,
And live, if I will, fingering my fingers
And throwing yesterday in the basket.
I am beset with reasonableness,
Swallow much that I know to be grass,
Tip as earth tips and not from dizziness.
But do not call me false.
What, must I turn shrew
Because I know what I know,
Wipe out the riverfront
Because it stinks of water?
I cannot do what there is not to do.
And what there is to do
Let me do somewhat crookedly,
Lest I speak too plain and everlasting
For such weather-vanes of understanding.

5.

Therefore, since all is well,
Come you no nearer than the barrel-organ
That I curse off to the next square
And there love, when I hear it not.
For I have a short, kind temper
And would spare while I can.
While the season fades and lasts
I would be old-fashioned with it.
I would be persuaded it is so,
Go mad to see it run, as it were horses,
Then be unmaddened, find it done,
Summon you close, a memory long gone.

So I am human, of much that is no more
Or never was, and in a moment
(I must hurry) it will be nineteen twenty-eight,
An old eternity pleading refutal.

Rejoice, Liars

Rejoice, the witch of truth has perished
Of her own will –
Falling to earth humanly
And rising in petty pain.

It was the last grandeur,
When the witch crashed
And had a mortal laming.

And quick heart turned to blood
Those fires of speculation
Where she burned long and coldly.

Away, flattery, she has lost pride.
Away, book-love, she has a body.
Away, body-love, she has a death
To be born into, an end to make
Of that eternity and grandeur
In which a legend pines till it comes true –
When fawning devil boasts belief
And the witch, for her own honour,
Takes on substance, shedding phantomness.

Beyond

Pain is impossible to describe
Pain is the impossibility of describing
Describing what is impossible to describe
Which must be a thing beyond description
Beyond description not to be known
Beyond knowing but not mystery
Not mystery but pain not plain but pain
But pain beyond but here beyond

In Due Form

I do not doubt you.
I know you love me.
It is a fact of your indoor face,
A true fancy of your muscularity.
Your step is confident.
Your look is thorough.
Your stay-beside-me is a pillow
To roll over on
And sleep as on my own upon.

But make me a statement
In due form on endless foolscap
Witnessed before a notary
And sent by post, registered,
To be signed for on receipt
And opened under oath to believe;
An antique paper missing from my strong-box,
A bond to clutch when hail tortures the chimney
And lightning circles redder round the city,
And your brisk step and thorough look
Are gallant but uncircumstantial,
And not mentionable in a doom-book.

Come, Words, Away

Come, words, away from mouths,
Away from tongues in mouths
And reckless hearts in tongues
And mouths in cautious heads —

Come, words, away to where
The meaning is not thickened
With the voice's fretting substance,
Nor look of words is curious
As letters in books staring out
All that man ever thought strange
And laid to sleep on white
Like the archaic manuscript
Of dreams at morning blacked on wonder.

Come, words, away to miracle
More natural than written art.
You are surely somewhat devils,
But I know a way to soothe
The whirl of you when speech blasphemes
Against the silent half of language
And, labouring the blab of mouths,
You tempt prolixity to ruin.
It is to fly you home from where
Like stealthy angels you made off once
On errands of uncertain mercy:
To tell with me a story here
Of utmost mercy never squandered
On niggard prayers for eloquence —
The marvelling on man by man.

I know a way, unwild we'll mercy
And spread the largest news
Where never a folded ear dare make
A deaf division of entirety.

That fluent half-a-story
Chatters against this silence
To which, words, come away now
In an all-merciful despite

105

Of early silvered treason
To the golden all of storying.

We'll begin fully at the noisy end
Where mortal halving tempered mercy
To the shorn utterance of man-sense;
Never more than savageries
Took they from your bounty-book.

Not out of stranger-mouths then
Shall words unwind but from the voice
That haunted there like dumb ghost haunting
Birth prematurely, anxious of death.
Not ours those mouths long-lipped
To falsity and repetition
Whose frenzy you mistook
For loyal prophetic heat
To be improved but in precision.

Come, words, away –
That was an alien vanity,
A rash startling and a preening
That from truth's wakeful sleep parted
When she within her first stirred story-wise,
Thinking what time it was or would be
When voiced illumination spread:
What time, what words, what she then.

Come, words, away,
And tell with me a story here,
Forgetting what's been said already:
That hell of hasty mouths removes
Into a cancelled heaven of mercies
By flight of words back to this plan
Whose grace goes out in utmost rings
To bounds of utmost storyhood.

But never shall truth circle so
Till words prove language is
How words come from far sound away
Through stages of immensity's small
Centering the utter telling
In truth's first soundlessness.

Come, words, away:
I am a conscience of you
Not to be held unanswered past
The perfect number of betrayal.
It is a smarting passion
By which I call –
Wherein the calling's loathsome as
Memory of man-flesh over-fondled
With words like over-gentle hands.
Then come, words, away,
Before lies claim the precedence of sin
And mouldered mouths writhe to outspeak us.

As to a Frontispiece

If you will choose the portrait,
I will write the work accordingly.
A German countenance
I could dilate on lengthily,
Punctilio and passion blending
To that slow national degree.

Or, if you wish more brevity
And have the face in mind –
A tidy creature, perhaps American –
I could provide a facile text,
The portrait being like enough
To stand for anyone.

But if you can't make up your mind
What poetry should look like,
What name to call for,
I think I have the very thing
If you can read without a picture
And postpone the frontispiece till later.

That is, as you may guess,
I have a work but, I regret,
No preliminary portrait.
Yet, if you can forgo one,
We may between us illustrate
This subsequent identity.

Tale of Modernity

1.

Shakespeare knew Lust by day,
With raw unsleeping eye.
And he cried, 'All but Truth I see,
Therefore Truth is, for Lust alone I see.'

By night Lust most on other men
Its swollen pictures shone.
And the sun brought shame, and they arose
Their hearts night-stained, but faces lustless.

They in the sun to themselves seemed well.
The sun in guise of Truth gave pardon.
Hypocrisy of seeming well
Blamed the sore visions on bed and night.

But Shakespeare knew Lust by day,
By day he saw his night, and he cried,
'O sexual sun, back into my loins,
Be night also, as you are.'

2.

Shakespeare distinguished: earth the obscure,
The sun the bold, the moon the hidden –
The sun speechless, earth a muttering,
The moon a whispering, white, smothered.

Bishop Modernity, to his spent flock cried,
'She is illusion, let her fade.'
And she, illusion and not illusion,
A sapphire being fell to earth, time-struck.

In colour live and liquid and earth-pale,
Never so near she, never so distant.
Never had time been futured so,
All reckoning on one fast page.

Time was a place where earth had been.
The whole past met there, she with it.
Truth seemed love grown cool as a brow,
And young as the moon, grown girl to self.

3.
Bishop Modernity plucked out his heart.
No agony could prove him Christ,
No lust could speak him honest Shakespeare.
A greedy frost filled where had been a heart.

And that disdainful age his flock,
Resolved against the dream-delight
Of soft succession another world to that,
Like woman slipping quiet into monk-thoughts,

Went in triumph of mind from the chapel,
Proud interior of voided breast,
To Heaven out, or Hell, or any name
That carnal sanctity bestows.

Home they went to heartless memories of wives
And appetites of whoredoms stilled
In lustful shaking off lust,
Of knowledge-gall, love's maddening part.

4.
Bishop Modernity in the fatal chapel watched
And end-of-time intoned as the Red Mass
Of man's drinking of the blood of man:
In quenched immunity he looked on her

Who from the fallen moon scattered the altar
With thin rays of challenged presence –
The sun put out here, and the lamps of time
Smoking black consternation to new desire.

Then did that devilish chase begin:
Bishop Modernity's heart plucked out
In old desire flew round against and toward her –
And he but shackled mind, to pulpit locked.

Which stirred up Shakespeare from listening tomb,
Who broke the lie and seized the maid, crying,
'Thou Bishop Double-Nothing, chase thy soul –
Till then she's ghost with me thy ghostly whole!'

As Many Questions as Answers

What is to start?
It is to have feet to start with.
What is to end?
It is to have nothing to start again with,
And not to wish.

What is to see?
It is to know in part.
What is to speak?
It is to add part to part
And make a whole
Of much or little.
What is to whisper?
It is to make soft
The greed of speaking faster
Than is substance for.
What is to cry out?
It is to make gigantic
Where speaking cannot last long.

What is to be?
It is to bear a name.
What is to die?
It is to be name only.
And what is to be born?
It is to choose the enemy self
To learn impossibility from.
And what is to have hope?
Is it to choose a god weaker than self,
And pray for compliments?

What is to ask?
It is to find an answer.
What is to answer?
Is it to find a question?

Earth

Have no wide fears for Earth:
Its universal name is 'Nowhere'.
If it is Earth to you, that is your secret.
The outer records leave off there,
And you may write it as it seems,
And as it seems, it is,
A seeming stillness
Amidst seeming speed.

Heavens unseen, or only seen,
Dark or bright space, unearthly space,
Is a time before Earth was
From which you inward move
Toward perfect now.

Almost the place it is not yet,
Potential here of everywhere –
Have no wide fears for it:
Its destiny is simple,
To be further what it will be.

Earth is your heart
Which has become your mind
But still beats ignorance
Of all it knows –
As miles deny the compact present
Whose self-mistrusting past they are.
Have no wide fears for Earth:
Destruction only on wide fears shall fall.

The Way It Is

It falls to an idiot to talk wisely.
It falls to a sot to wear beauty.
It falls to many to be blessed
In their shortcomings,
As to the common brute it falls
To see real miracles
And howl with irksome joy.

Many are the confusions that fall,
Many are the inspired ones.
Much is there indeed contrary,
Much is there indeed wonderful.
A most improbable one it takes
To tell what is so,
And the strangest creature of all
To be natural.

The Wind, the Clock, the We

The wind has at last got into the clock –
Every minute for itself.
There's no more sixty,
There's no more twelve,
It's as late as it's early.

The rain has washed out the numbers.
The trees don't care what happens.
Time has become a landscape
Of suicidal leaves and stoic branches –
Unpainted as fast as painted.
Or perhaps that's too much to say,
With the clock devouring itself
And the minutes given leave to die.

The sea's no picture at all.
To sea, then: that's time now,
And every mortal heart's a sailor
Sworn to vengeance on the wind,
To hurl life back into the thin teeth
Out of which first it whistled,
An idiotic defiance of it knew not what
Screeching round the studying clock.

Now there's neither ticking nor blowing.
The ship has gone down with its men,
The sea with the ship, the wind with the sea.
The wind at last got into the clock,
The clock at last got into the wind,
The world at last got out of itself.

At last we can make sense, you and I,
You lone survivors on paper,
The wind's boldness and the clock's care
Become a voiceless language,
And I the story hushed in it –
Is more to say of me?
Do I say more than self-choked falsity
Can repeat word for word after me,
The script not altered by a breath
Of perhaps meaning otherwise?

The World and I

This is not exactly what I mean
Any more than the sun is the sun.
But how to mean more closely
If the sun shines but approximately?
What a world of awkwardness!
What hostile implements of sense!
Perhaps this is as close a meaning
As perhaps becomes such knowing.
Else I think the world and I
Must live together as strangers and die –
A sour love, each doubtful whether
Was ever a thing to love the other.
No, better for both to be nearly sure
Each of each – exactly where
Exactly I and exactly the world
Fail to meet by a moment, and a word.

The Flowering Urn

And every prodigal greatness
Must creep back into strange home,
Must fill the hollow matrix of
The never-begotten perfect son
Who never can be born.

And every quavering littleness
Must shrink more tinily than it knows
Into the giant hush whose sound
Reverberates within itself
As tenderest numbers cannot improve.

And from this jealous secrecy
Will rise itself, will flower up
The likeness kept against false seed:
When death-whole is the seed
And no new harvest to fraction sowing.

Will rise the same peace that held
Before fertility's lie awoke
The virgin sleep of Mother All:
The same but for the way in flowering
It speaks of fruits that could not be.

Nor Is It Written

Nor is it written that you may not grieve.
There is no rule of joy, long may you dwell
Not smiling yet in that last pain,
On that last supper of the heart.
It is not written that you must take joy
Because not thus again shall you sit down
To ply the mingled banquet
Which the deep larder of illusion shed
Like myth in time grown not astonishing.
Lean to the cloth awhile, and yet awhile,
And even may your eyes caress
Proudly the used abundance.
It is not written in what heart
You may not pass from magic plenty
Into the straitened nowadays.
To each is given secrecy of heart,
To make himself what heart he please
In stirring up from that fond table
To sit him down at this sharp meal.
It shall not here be asked of him
'What thinks your heart?'
Long may you sorely to yourself upbraid
This truth unwild, this only-bread.
It is not counted what large passions
Your heart in ancient private keeps alive.
To each is given what defeat he will.

Auspice of Jewels

They have connived at those jewelled fascinations
That to our hands and arms and ears
And heads and necks and feet
And all the winding stalk
Extended the mute spell of the face.

They have endowed the whole of us
With such a solemn gleaming
As in the dark of flesh-love
But the face at first did have.
We are studded with wide brilliance
As the world with towns and cities –
The travelling look builds capitals
Where the evasive eye may rest
Safe from the too immediate lodgement.

Obscure and bright these forms
Which as the women of their lingering thought
In slow translucence we have worn.
And the silent given glitter locks us
In a not false unplainness:
Have we ourselves been sure
What steady countenance to turn them?

Until now – when this passionate neglect
Of theirs, and our twinkling reluctance,
Are like the reader and the book
Whose fingers and whose pages have confided
But whose sight and sense
Meet in a chilly time of strangeness;
And it is once more early, anxious,
And so late, it is intolerably the same
Not speaking coruscation
That both we and they made endless, dream-long,
Lest be cruel to so much love
The closer shine of waking,
And what be said sound colder
Than the ghastly love-lisp.

Until now – when to go jewelled
We must despoil the drowsy masquerade
Where gloom of silk and gold
And glossy dazed adornments
Kept safe from flagrant realness
The forgeries of ourselves we were –
When to be alive as love feigned us
We must steal death and its wan splendours
From the women of their sighs we were.

For we are now otherwise luminous.
The light which was spent in jewels
Has performed upon the face
A gradual eclipse of recognition.
We have passed from plaintive visibility
Into total rareness,
And from this reunion of ourselves and them
Under the snuffed lantern of time
Comes an astonished flash like truth
Or the unseen-unheard entrance of someone
Whom eyes and ears in their dotage
Have forgotten for dead or lost.

(And hurrying towards distracted glory,
Gemmed lady-pageants, bells on their hearts,
By restless knights attended
Whose maudlin plumes and pommels
Urge the adventure past return.)

Memories of Mortalities

1.
My Mother and My Birth

My mother was a snake, but warm:
In her a welling heart, spite unfrozen.
Hating, she loved.
Coiling to choke, she kissed.

And men were done then
Slowing in same doom-pause,
Same morrow of old sun.
They were about their deaths then –
They were worn, then, men,
To scant remainders of themselves,
And their kinds were fatal:
As comes the flowering-day
When seedlings take their names
And are the final things –
Which in their labelled promise
Seemed the first giant garden
Where beauty is such tropic horror
That death to make fright's suddenness
And self-sensation is not needful.

It being then such lateness
Of world, death-season,
Flowering, name-taking,
The cold snake to its melting came –
She was Contempt of Time,
That Spirit which at Origin
Bittered against the taste false-sweet
Of Future, on her lightning tongue
Already poison and corrupted Past.
This was my mother,
Who, when the mortal lag took haste
And death became contemporary,
Turned fond, and loved the flesh despised –
As ghouls the living love,
Their griefs claiming, adoring their disease.

Hers was the paradox I chose
To have heretic body of:
I, Spirit which at End
Greets remnant Now, to make
Beginning, in this prompt decline,
Of death's all-soon respited day,
Which, dawning infinite from death
Like night from night, encompasses
Entirety in its utter light:
This Self of Subsequence
To Time personally structured,
Touched, touching, minded, minding,
Interbreathing, interbreathed:
I, smalled laterness than Time,
My double-tongued snake-mother's singler meaning.

And it was idiot nature,
There to be babe, outfrowning from unborn,
And there to suckle swooning,
Giddy with dreadful newness of myself,
Clutching the stranger-breast
As shipwrecked orphan chooses
One stranger from the rest for friend,
By logic of confusion and by need
Of privacy against the many.

So fallible that nature:
For, being, I was none of her,
And she, delivered of me, held
No backward life of mine.
That union in material magic –
Her larger-than-herself, untrue extreme,
With my so smaller-than-self leastness –
Had magic's aftermath,
Materiality's division:
As if it had not been,
And she to snakehood's tears again,
And I to opposite sense of death –
Who yet an early flesh could have
Because Contempt of Time, relenting
On Time's sickness of time,
Grew time-like, stayed death's full succession.

For, in this mock-beneficence,
Regret, aged Nothingness, took change
And was dissolving Everything –
By whose sophistry of flesh with spirit
Twilight-same, I argued me a body,
A flesh-prelude to myself,
With ancestry in snake-slough cast
Like silence from loud dumbness.

Oh, obscure!
Birth, body, is by darkness,
And mine by that opacity
Which, being death's late dawn,
Looms mystery-bright at truth-verge.
This night-time that I wage,
My temporal person, prophet of myself
In lazy mouth's futurities,
Must live, precede me mortally,
That I inherit of myself
By refutation of those semblances
Which liker, liker, are less like
To ultimate me as I remember
Oh, how not-like all to this survival
Of myself, this very-me made last
Of strange approximation to myself
In eager hesitancies –
Lest quickness of me be too instant,
And I but the unproven echo
Of dispersed original.

Therefore such quickness as makes life,
The stuttering slow grammaring of self
That death with memoried seeming crowns.
And were I otherwise myself
Than in a near-mistaken mask's
Gradual fading into true-face,
Then were I no fit face to welcome
Gradual Now familiarly to death,
No visible pied voice to mingle
Natural with garish hearing,
No idiom of life-translation
Leading Time to after-dwelling,

No almost-lie to warrant truth by,
No long event of me by which
To contradict eventfulness –
Oh, Contradiction,
World-being, human condition,
Stolen grace, outrage unfinal:
What farthest Next is End,
Composure, whole Cessation?
Nearer and nearer Next, till Now,
The measure over-fine, impossible,
Contradiction's life-length
Cut to the moment which is life and death
In one unlivable solution.
Then comes pure death, the grace compelled,
Duration cleansed of day-change.

In such rhythm of nearness, nextness, nowness,
From present arrestation borne a motion
Motionless toward present progress,
Thus I in fellowed dying walked
To Subsequence – taking the numerous path
That Time had greatly narrowed to,
Arriving there as at a home
General to all who dare be so undone,
Save for mortality remembered.

2.
My Father and My Childhood

As childhood is to fairies, fancies,
Briefness of thought, and of heart
Fast change from hot to cool –
A flickering purpose, wild, then weak,
First passion, then a fear and pouting
Of clumsy fingers told, and spent
In clumsy shadows, petulances
Spread in swollen tear-mist:
By such uncertain tides

I lived those doubtful years a child –
When to be live was half-felt sting
Of destiny, and half-stirred sleep of chance.
That was the time of tales –
Rising of mind to fragmentary hours
And fleshward fall by night
To scarce roused sloth of self.

For which I took a fox to father.
From many grinning tales he came
Sorrowed to that lonely burrow
Where the snake my mother left me
Cruelly to find what world I might
To history in, to get my name of.
There came the fox my father,
Between the tales to ponder, speak
The gruff philosophies of foxes:
'All is mistrust and mischief,
Bestiality and bestial comfort.
Life is a threadbare fiction –
Large the holes and thin the patches.
The gainer is the loser;
For to gain is to gain wisdom,
And wisdom's riches are the monies
In which poverty is counted –
To know how poor, how less than full
The gaping treasuries of truth,
Where's lack, what's niggard, which the fattened lie.'
Oh, famished fox-wit –
Hunger stanched with taste of hunger,
Shammed meals and cunning feints
And wily shifts to make one morrow more
Of failing fortune, duplication
Sour of sweets remembered sour.

Forth we went, this paternality
In careworn foxhood scrupulous
To teach the public pomp and private woes
Of social nature, crossed estate
Where reason's loud with nonsense
And nonsense soft with truth –
And I, droll pertinacity

To turn the random child-head round
In sphering wonder-habit
And step new-footed fervour
On whatever ground like books lay
To my learning docile, garrulous,
A world of self-blind pages,
Staring to be read.

Whether the misery more those tales
Through town and village scampering
With beggar-cry, to operatic heavens
From hoarse house-tops venting
Weather-vane conclusions, jangled morals,
Spasmed glees and glooms and thunders –
Or that from town to village countrywide
Homeless we stalked the straggling world,
Pursuing laws of change and sameness
To their momentary finish in
Equivocation's false repose –
Whether the plight more ours,
My father's, in his fox-despair
Driving that unlaughed laughter to hard grief,
A bigot brooding, fortitude
Of losses and mis-hoping,
And mine, in restive after-hope
Protracting death's impulsion of mere death
Till might be death-exceeding courage,
Perchance a love or loves to overreach
Time's mete of forwardness
And break with me the life-fast –
Or whether theirs more sorry burden,
That they built to heights and stretches
Direly not sufficing to be that
They climbed to, walked on, boasted
Sight-substantial, likely, thinkable,
Were countered in their caution
By stumblings, crumblings, mysteries
And mishaps disaccording
With their miserly assurance –

We did not make division
Between the world's calamitous revolving
And our sore travel with it
On roads toward starved renewal curved.
One bounden omen then the whole,
Community of presages
Not yet in strict dissemblance parted:
My mother's tears afall like leaves
The wind takes, not the earth,
Being upon the branch already dust;
My father's dour world-worrying,
The fabled fox into humaneness come
With stealthy nose and cynic tread
But smile less proud than anciently
When Time was less the common theme
And more the learned axiom;
The world's tossed mind, a ghost-sea
In dying deluge breaking
On all the secret shores of thought
Risen against Time's drowned horizon;
And I my living variance
From livingness, of death-kind
Live protagonist, whose mouth's 'to-day'
With morrows folded in from morrows
Hung speechlessly enwrapped.

And was it childhood, then,
From snake to fox's patronage,
And tortured idling, twisted course
Between the hither-thither stagger
Of the universal doom-day?
But was not childhood ever thus?
A premonition trembling distant
On lips of language shy,
Fast futures there acrowd
And quieted with story-book retard –
Even as I those troubled times of father
To story took and, parrying conclusion,
My fair curls shadowed among tales,
Made Imminence a dream-hush
Whose vocal waking slept inside my own.

127

3.
Sickness and Schooling

The later griping, when we suffer mind-woes –
This was once lesser pain of flesh:
'It hurts,' we cried, 'it seems to hurt.
Some something loves me not,
I am not loved – and where to fly
And what if not myself to be?
Is there a better I than this
Which Teacher Pain would not so pinch?'
We toss in hot self-inquisition.
It is our bed, the sweat and shivering
Are greatly ours, the Doctor's smile
Means that the world expects this very me
To be myself against what others choose:
The world is many, we are many,
And none the other loves so well
That to be lovable is to be loved.
And Nurse reads on: Jack scrambles toward the top.
I cannot scream 'Don't go!'
The little Mermaid starts to float to heaven.
'I won't! I won't!' My legs keep sinking.
And then I sleep.
Nurse does not really care.
I care, I wake up well.

The lasting woes return the heart
To early sickness – oh, to be ill as then
And wake up well.
But the heart finds an empty schoolroom,
No child to be sent home,
No feverish bedside to embrace
The lonely nightmare –
It is no nightmare, but a realness
Like a name and face perhaps oneself.
And the bed is cold.
And the heart is many dreams by day
Which sleep instructs us of:
We wake up wiser but not well,
Not having fallen ill. Yesterday
We were not ill, to-day

We are but older in those woes
By which we have grown kind to pain,
Feeling it not, since we are many
And it must be so. We may not grieve
That life is much and numerous –
Since we live, and must be many.
We have learnt to know and to be known,
And no more ask for love.
Grief is a soft decorum now
Of usedness to love-lack.
The world is broken into knowledges,
And every part an undisputed woe is:
We dare not grieve, lest something fall away
And with it take ourselves.

Thus we make fast the world
And each a charge of numbers lays
Upon the haughty child each was
Once when the heart did nearly close
Against ordeal of numbers.
Oh, we have learnt.
Not one has never been to school,
Not come away a tearless devil
Whom the world has won to membership
In cordial hellishness.
Not one has ever found
The learning of gregarious profusion
For just so many years not stead of wisdom,
Not dear to hungry mind, consumable
For just so many years
Till wisdom was, and worldliness
Became the shadow of unjoy:
Through which our joy had need to pass
To reach the shining thoughts –
As heaven is a sight withheld,
Erratic among clouds,
If the eyes have not first dwelt
Thickly on what's near to see,
Hidden the rarer visions dark in time,
There to be sobered and attain
Numbered appearance with the common things
That also wait their hour of light.

We have been to school.
The world is many, we have learnt.
Neither together nor alone live we.
It is a ragged union,
As insecure as close.
We have learnt to do little, be little,
And to preserve intenser self
For a last excellence of world
That may not be, or cannot.
I have been to school, as all.
I was apprenticed to my time
And in the craft of contemporaneity
Grew accurate, and by the rule
Of then-and-now I babbled
The abrupt opinion, shuffled
Between what was and is
Like any nonchalant of taught experience.

'Know!' they said
And I knew.
The child grew girl of current kind.
I was obedient to my world,
I learnt to know the frown from the pursed smile,
I won the prizes which are won
By future citizens, trained dogs of wisdom –
A plaster Dante and a leather Browning
And, at the high degree of slavishness,
That stare of dire approval
Which follows good behaviour to its grave.

Having no mirror of my own,
Being by nature superstitious
Of what's mine and not,
I had not looked to claim
A featured someone for myself.
But the world pressed a mirror on my shyness.
'Not shy,' to the no one in that mirror
I not self-recognized protested:
Not shy, but that not claimed by my own mirror –
Which I had not yet –
The seemly schoolroom countenance
Glassed like a wretched anyone

In the great overcast reflection
For just so many years my world.

I had been old.
Oh, hateful wizened youth,
Those just so many years
Of feigned astuteness, false incognito.
For it was not a guise of me,
It was a world without me,
As if I came into a room of strangers
And found myself not there,
And was a stranger,
By the law of courtesy which governs
Foreign presence, sudden stranding
In a place where one remains
About to go, about to go.

Did I fall ill again at last,
That I am now younger than then?
And have the little mirror which is mine
And make in it an image which I greet
Without a shudder, no, with even joy?
A joy of being as the first time myself
And reckless what my world decides –
Whether I am co-native or a trespasser
From the dread death-wrapt province
On live existence bent?

I fell forgetful.
Having been taught to suffer,
To be one among the many,
To go like leper in a world of lepers,
I became expert in equivocation,
Safe in my outer ways from being overheard
In candid converse with myself.

'I cannot now,' I said, 'offend.
I have the civil marks, my story must
Stand in the books next theirs.
What will they write of me?'
I fell forgetful, I fell curious.
What will they write of me?

They wrote nothing different, of course.
I saw that I should have to go back
And write my story myself.
But not to school.
At school we learnt to write nothing different.
But not to childhood,
Not to be ill, requiring of the world
A love of me it could not have,
Too made of many to allow
More than the passing love for each.
I should have to go back.
I must find somewhere to go back to
Like a life to live.

I fell forgetful.
I had learnt to be silent
And yet to be.
I had learnt how the world speaks.
I fell forgetful of speaking.
But had I continued to say nothing,
Nothing different, I should have died:
They would have written nothing different.
So I began to live.
It was outrageous,
I made mortal mistakes,
I did not mean to live so mortally.

But something must be written about me,
And not by them.
So I began those mistold confidences
Which now read like profanity of self
To my internal eye
And which my critic hand erases
As the story grows too different to speak of
In the way the world speaks.

Be Grave, Woman

Be grave, woman for love
Still hungering as gardens
For rain though flowerless
What perfume now to rise
From weary expectation.

Be not wild to love,
Poor witch of mysteries
Whose golden age thy body's
Alchemy aburn was
Unto haggard ember.

Beauty's flesh to phantom
Wears unprosperous
And come but devils of
Chill omen to adore
The perforce chaste idolon.

Be grave, woman, to greet
The kiss, the clasp, the shudder which
Rage of thee from crafty
Lust unrolls – and think
These are thy dead to grieve on

And thyself the death in whom
Love must disaster and
Be long ago in ruin-sweet
Story, on the sense to ponder
Thou alone, stark mind.

Divestment of Beauty

She, she and she and she –
Which of these is not lovely?
In her long robe of glamour now
And her beauty like a ribbon tied
The wisdom of her head round?

To call these 'women'
Is homage of the eye:
Such sights to greet as natural,
Such beings to proclaim
Companion to expectance.

But were they now who take
This gaudy franchise from
The accolade of stilted vision
Their lady-swaddlings to unwrap
And shed the timorous scales of nakedness –

It were a loathsome spectacle, you think?
Eventual entrails of deity
Worshipful eye offending?
It were the sign, man,
To pluck the loathsome eye,

Forswear the imbecile
Theology of loveliness,
Be no more doctor in antiquities –
Chimeras of the future
In archaic daze embalmed –

And grow to later youth,
Felling the patriarchal leer
That it lie reft of all obscenities
While she and she, she, she, disclose
The recondite familiar to your candour.

Wishing More Dear

Can this finding your presence dear,
And also wishing mine found dear,
And hoarding under courtesy
Fancied minutiae of affection –
Can this be made somewhat of lust
That, clamorous for loving signs,
My heart so piously disowns
Thought of the usual embraces?

The morning's memory of lust
Is bashful and the naked dream
Clothed with denial in its telling.
What lewd unspeakable confession
Holds up the honesty between us
Like dream which better had been told,
That, risking candour's horrid blush,
I greet you with too fond a look?

After So Much Loss

After so much loss –
Seeming of gain,
Seeming of loss –
Subsides the swell of indignation
To the usual rhythm of the year.

The coward primroses are up,
We contract their profuse mildness.
Women with yet a few springs to live
Clutch them in suppliant bouquets
On the way to relatives,
Who, no, do not begrudge
This postponement of funerals.
And, oh, how never tired, and tired,
The world of primroses, how spring
The bended spirit fascinates
With promise of revival,
Leaving more honest summer to proclaim
That this is all – a brighter disappointment –
Time has to give to an implacable
Persuasion of things lost, wrongly.

Is it to wonder, then,
That we defy the unsuspecting moment,
Release our legs from the year's music,
And, to the reckless strum of hate,
Dance – grinding from primroses the tears
They never of themselves would have shed?
None dances whom no hate stirs,
Who has not lost and loathed the loss,
Who does not feel deprived.
Slyest rebellion of the feet,
The chaste and tremulous disport
Of children, limbs in passionless wave –
None dances whom no hate stirs,
Or shall not stir.

As sure as primrosed spring betides,
After so much loss,
The hate will out, the dance be on,
And many of their rage fall down.
It is easy as spring to yield to the year,
And easy as dance to break with the year.
But to go with the year in partition
Between seeming loss, seeming gain,
That is the difficult decorum.
Nor are the primroses unwelcome.

When Love Becomes Words

The yet undone, become the unwritten
By the activity of others
And the immobile pen of ourselves
Lifted, in postponed readiness,
Over the yet unsmooth paper of time –
Themes of the writing-table now,
All those implicit projects
By our minds rescued from enactment,
That lost literature which only death reads.

And we expect works of one another
Of exceeding not so much loveliness
Or fame among our physical sighs
As quietness, eventful
Not beyond thought, which moves unstrangely,
Without the historic sword-flash.

And I shall say to you, 'There is needed now
A poem upon love, to forget the kiss by
And be more love than kiss to the lips.'
Or, failing your heart's talkativeness,
I shall write this spoken kiss myself,
Imprinting it on the mouth of time
Perhaps too finally, but slowly,
Since execution now is prudent
With the reflective sleep the tongue takes
Between thought and said.

Thus, at last, to instruct ourselves
In the nothing we are now doing,
These unnatural days of inaction,
By telling the thing in a natural tone.
We must be brave:
Daring the sedentary future
With no other hope of passion than words,
And finding what we feel in what we think,
And knowing the rebated sentiment
For the wiser age of a once foolish deed.
As to say, where I once might have risen,
Bent to kiss like a blind wind searching

For a firm mouth to discover its own,
I now sit sociably in the chair of love,
Happy to have you or someone facing
At the distance bought by the lean of my head;
And then, if I may, go to my other room
And write of a matter touching all matters
With a compact pressure of room
Crowding the world between my elbows;
Further, to bed, and soft,
To let the night conclude, my lips still open,
That a kiss has been, or other thing to dream.
The night was formerly the chronicler,
Whispering lewd rumours to the morning.
But now the story of the evening
Is the very smile of supper and after,
Is not infant to the nurse Romance,
Is the late hour at which I or you
May have written or read perhaps even this.

Sometimes we shall declare falsely,
Young in an earlier story-sense
Impossible at the reduced hour of words.
But however we linger against exactness,
Enlarging the page by so much error
From the necessities of chance survived,
We cannot long mistake ourselves,
Being quit now of those gestures
Which made the world a tale elastic,
Of no held resemblance to our purpose.
For we have meant, and mean, but one
Consensus of experience,
Notwithstanding the difference in our names
And that we have seemed to be born
Each to a changing plot and loss
Of feeling (though our earth it is)
At home in such a timeward place.
We cannot now but match our words
With a united nod of recognition –
We had not, hitherto, heard ourselves speak
For the garrulous vigour and furore
Of the too lively loves as they clattered
Like too many letters from our hasty lips.

It is difficult to remember
That we are doing nothing,
Are to do nothing, wish to do nothing.
From a spurious cloud of disappointment
We must extract the sincere drop of relief
Corresponding to the tear in our thoughts
That we have no reason to shed.
We are happy.
These engagements of the mind,
Unproductive of the impulse to kiss,
Ring to the heart like love essential,
Safe from theatric curiosity
Which once directed our desires
To an end of gaudy shame and flourish,
So that we played these doleful parts
Abandoned between fright and pomp.

There is now little to see
And yet little to hide.
The writing of 'I love you'
Contains the love if not entirely
At least with lovingness enough
To make the rest a shadow round us
Immaculately of shade
Not love's hallucinations substanced.
It is truer to the heart, we know now,
To say out than to secrete the bold alarm,
Flushed with timidity's surprises,
That looms between the courage to love
And the habit of groping for results.

The results came first, our language
Bears the scars of them: we cannot
Speak of love but the lines lisp
With the too memorable accent,
Endearing what, instead of love, we love-did.
First come the omens, then the thing we mean.
We did not mean the gasp or hotness;
This is no cooling, stifling back
The bannered cry love waved before us once.
That was a doubt, and a persuasion –
By the means of believing, with doubt's art,

What we were, in our stubbornness, least sure of.
There is less to tell of later
But more to say.
There are, in truth, no words left for the kiss.
We have ourselves to talk of;
And the passing characters we were –
Nervous of time on the excitable stage –
Surrender to their lasting authors
That we may study, still alive,
What love or utterance shall preserve us
From that other literature
We fast exerted to perpetuate
The mortal chatter of appearance.

Think not that I am stern
To banish now the kiss, ancient,
Or how our hands or cheeks may brush
When our thoughts have a love and a stir
Short of writable and a grace
Of not altogether verbal promptness.
To be loving is to lift the pen
And use it both, and the advance
From dumb resolve to the delight
Of finding ourselves not merely fluent
But ligatured in the embracing words
Is by the metaphor of love,
And still a cause of kiss among us,
Though kiss we do not – or so knowingly,
The taste is lost in the taste of the thought.

Let us not think, in being so protested
To the later language and condition,
That we have ceased to love.
We have ceased only to become – and are.
Few the perplexities, the intervals
Allowed us of shy hazard:
We could not if we would be rash again,
Take the dim loitering way
And stumble on till reason like a horse
Stood champing fear at the long backward turn,
And we the sorry rider, new to the mount,
Old to the fugitive manner.

But dalliance still rules our hearts
In the name of conscience. We raise our eyes
From the immediate manuscript
To find a startled present blinking the past
With sight disfigured and a brow reproachful,
Pointing the look of time toward memory
As if we had erased the relics
In order to have something to write on.
And we leave off, for the length of conscience,
Discerning in the petulant mist
The wronged face of someone we know,
Hungry to be saved from rancour of us.
And we love: we separate the features
From the fading and compose of them
A likeness to the one that did not wait
And should have waited, learned to wait.
We raise our eyes to greet ourselves
With a conviction that none is absent
Or none should be, from the domestic script of words
That reads out welcome to all who we are.

And then to words again
After – was it – a kiss or exclamation
Between face and face too sudden to record.
Our love being now a span of mind
Whose bridge not the droll body is
Striding the waters of disunion
With sulky grin and groaning valour,
We can make love miraculous
As joining thought with thought and a next,
Which is done not by crossing over
But by knowing the words for what we mean.
We forbear to move, it seeming to us now
More like ourselves to keep the written watch
And let the reach of love surround us
With the warm accusation of being poets.

Doom in Bloom

Now flower the oldest seeds.
The secret of the root no more
Keeps jealous distance from the air.
The dark intent, so lothfully ascending,
At last to resolution grows;
The glance of long reluctance shows.

Weakly we write upon
The closing surface of oblivion.
Our faith in earth, in nether sameness,
Hurries to take the separate colour.
And leaning on the faded air
We flaunt ourselves against despair.

Gruesomely joined in hate
Of unlike efflorescence,
We were a cruel compacted silence
From which unlovable centuries sprang.
But time has knit so hard a crust
That speak and differ now we must –

Or be in pride encased
Until the living way has ceased
And only death comes to occur.
Though half our zeal but fair is,
Spells but an earth's variety,
Hope makes a stronger half to beauty

When from the deep bed torn
Of ultimate misgiving
An auspice of like peril to bring.
The lone defiance blossoms failure,
But risk of all by all beguiles
Fate's wreckage into similar smiles.

Nothing So Far

Nothing so far but moonlight
Where the mind is;
Nothing in that place, this hold,
To hold;
Only their faceless shadows to announce
Perhaps they come –
Nor even do they know
Whereto they cast them.

Yet here, all that remains
When each has been the universe:
No universe, but each, or nothing.
Here is the future swell curved round
To all that was.

What were we, then,
Before the being of ourselves began?
Nothing so far but strangeness
Where the moments of the mind return.
Nearly, the place was lost
In that we went to stranger places.

Nothing so far but nearly
The long familiar pang
Of never having gone;
And words below a whisper which
If tended as the graves of live men should be
May bring their names and faces home.

It makes a loving promise to itself,
Womanly, that there
More presences are promised
Than by the difficult light appear.
Nothing appears but moonlight's morning –
By which to count were as to strew
The look of day with last night's rid of moths.

Laura and Francisca

The Island, and Here

My name, as the title shows,
Is Laura, and hers Francisca.
And my age must be thirty,
As hers must be I should say six,
Judging by and judging by.

I will tell you everything.
On the island of Mallorca
Sometimes I see an English newspaper.
In one I read, a young man questioned
In the private question-corner,
'I want to go away and live abroad
On very, very little a day.'
The answer was, 'The cheapest climate,
Scenery and food are in Mallorca.'
But, Mr. Very Very Little A Day,
I live here, and I ought to know.
This is not heaven, but the smallest earth.
Beyond which comes perhaps *bon día tenga*
Or another same fiesta of San Juan,
But never more than what may please
Without dishonouring mortality.
Which is not to buy paradise
Through the low rate of exchange.
Money will buy you only money here,
Another same yourself, unmagicked
By the cheap touch of salvation.

Of course, a lot of people come here,
And Mr. Short at Palma finds them houses.
But there they end and end.
And that is why they like it here:
Wherever the soul gives in to flesh
Without a struggle is home.
But you, I think, did not ask your question
In the homely sense of tiredness.

145

But enough of you, this is a poem
About how Laura turned into Francisca.
And you come in only to show
Mallorca in this poem is not
A favoured island made for man by God,
But so much godliness as man has
In being faithful to being man.

There are many habitable islands.
To be habitable is an island:
The rest is space, childhood of the mind,
Where keeping house is statecraft:
The habiting mind seems to itself
Tremendous, as a child writes large.
Then comes maturity, and loss of size,
And continents give way to islands,
And keeping house is play –
A small circle of meaning
Within a larger, the larger being
Truth, by which man knows of man.
And so a refuge-island is only
A grinning hollow of sarcasm and despite:
Such is the goatish propaganda
Of uninhabitable Ireland.

England is knowledge's self-doubt:
Whatever lies beyond makes here
An island in a sea of there.
From England sailed shy heroes
To stretch an empire of interrogation
As far as man could think –
Without forgetting the way back to silence.
From Spain tortured grandees of resignation
Sent hope out to die nobly;
Its angry face from God hidden,
The Spanish triumph is a self-damned flesh.

Of islands speaks the Mediterranean.
Precociously the Cretans fashioned
A private idiom of death.
With Semite impartiality the Phoenicians
Mothered the strangers of the little places.

Which Athens taught their several minor prides.
Corsica, man of France, triumphed too well,
By littleness was great, and of greatness, nothing.
Malta, Italy of islands,
Dreaming of greatness won from fate
Only an aged bad temper.
I mention it because they say
It is an island not unlike Mallorca.
And so is one man like another.
Up the slow grade of resemblance creeps
Identity – till the exact image
Is unphenomenal.
Exact Mallorca, least everywhere,
Most earth-like miniature
Of a too heavenly planet:
Here is a day a day, a word a word,
Man only men, and God the future,
Too late a subject for to-day
And better given to to-morrow,
The eternal Sunday.

I got this out of no bazaar of views;
But, looking round for the last day,
I found the first, grown small and final
Against the imagined years
And narrowed into one same previousness.
And what's an end, but honest time
Confessing that it only came before?
Looking around for literal death,
I found such literal life:
Like Deyá, built within itself,
Never a step beyond – as the church leads
From Deyá hill to Deyá down,
The Baptist crying off who would go on
To angelhood and always
Without growing small by death in Deyá.

And so we came to Deyá,
A village of Mallorca,
The island of an island,
As the bodily look carries a face.
Exact Mallorca, minute Deyá,

147

Finest and only fraction
Of the sole integer.
From here, the first least measure,
Truth has the difference only of more
Between its least and most:
If you have lived a thorough death
And, being dead, know self as truth-same –
However less than truth, yet not less true.
(Less true is difference in life,
Walking the other way, toward fancy
And the opposite islands of nowhere.)

But I think this is enough to show
My poem is not travel whimsy,
Or that mind's masquerade called fiction,
But a poem, that is, a fact
Standing alone, an island,
A little all that more grows
According to the trouble you can take.
For here I tell you, instead of Laura,
The samest least of her, Francisca.
May you, after this briefest day,
Sleep the short sleep and, waking up,
Ask, 'Is this not yesterday
When it was to-day – and to-morrow,
The long present instead of night?'

II
Francisca, and Scarcely More

'Francisca will be wild – she sings.'
This is a way of looking at a child
With years of hate between.
Francisca is.
She witches now. I love her.

Where man accounts himself a poor creature
And woman loves him for no more –
Without need to account herself
In such slight reckonings –
Francisca tricks and none prevents.

For she is a child.
Her eyes with her unbroken face are smooth.
Her back in which she hides me
Makes her to dance with speckled hair
Through which but shows a sometimes violet frock
Or other happy death or witch's pallor.
And prettily she keeps the thing
That if truth spoke all-hearably,
And Francisca were not,
Were only blazing judgement,
And terrible to see.

But here's no need for judgement to be spoken:
That man which here unlives himself
In chance began, and in chance is saved –
Let through the doors of destiny
Without a word, never having sought
More than to be in death the same.
Here insignificance is grateful,
To have not marked itself for doom.
Here with the body falls off but the race,
And what's left is a man's own, then,
A private good – if this content him.

And so no need to think,
Walking the village up and round,
How shall such wisdoms be preserved
When peace, the slow-to-gather storm,
Sweeps in, which nothing can outlast
Except what never braved it
With fair-weather reasoning.
No need to think: already have survived
Such wisdoms by peace forecontracted,
Choosing their given mortal size
Against the victory over death
That makes great only, and not so.
No need to pity, walking in and past:
They have fed, and on the daily bread
Which fills instantly and again.

And so Francisca sails her boat
(I gave it her, she found it by the door)
Down the slow *'siqui* by the wall,
Looking up only not to talk.
She lets it ride, then catches up
By scarcely walking, teasing along
Until the boat at any moment
Might play the fool and drop into the hole.
Enough danger for a short voyage.
Then she turns out her basket.
Three cards to laugh at? someone else.
A sprig to smell? not now.
Has anything dropped out? perhaps.

This is the moment for me to pass,
The moment to be two:
I who am not, being otherwise
Than the laws of similarity
Allow legally otherwise,
And I who by a sleight of person
Trifle with my different likeness
To be Francisca to the different
Who are more otherwise than I.
Up to the letter-hour then,
A softening of the eyes to be far off
To the far-off, who know
No other near than their own farness,
In which they are immediate,
And, after, a future still more far.
For every distant envelope
Torn open in Deyá and containing
Apparently a letter, just arrived,
That's so much less of far.

Or Robert fetches.
What letters and what news?
By now he knows what will be he
In the already counted afterwards.
What letters and what news?
Alas, they sign themselves forever
A world that was.

150

Alas, Laura, the same yesterday.
They have not written, they have.
Alas and happily: the world fails,
Yet life still is, memory translated
Into the language of *not again*.
Laura restores the fact eclipsed
By the fact subsequent to the fact,
In which they had persuasion of time,
The lie that does as well as truth
For a time.

Francisca shakes her various hair
When Robert fetches and Deyá seems severe.
Francisca with soft presence
Looked strange and sang the other way,
Nor did she bashfully.
But the Madonna of Cas Pintat
Unnewly out of small, just eyes
Spoke as usual the comfort
Of the short day that by shortness
Lasts only long enough
For a day always, saved from change.
Dear Robert, therefore have no fear.
Comfort by degrees of pain not felt
Attests the world not world-like
Recovering from being the world.
Dear Robert, if you break,
Holding your living self of man
Against death's selfless person
Too triumphantly, no more is lost
Than time, the unrepeatable –
Man shall yet have outlived man,
Though in a mortal immortality
In Deyá, where Francisca witches,
Darkening the full of meaning
That the Madonna clarifies
In consumable part only
Across her passionless counter.

At any rate, sit down and rest now.
The basket was too heavy.
I'll put the rice into the tin
And sort the vegetables and letters.
From a world that was – alas.
And has the will surrendered
To impossibility at last,
Which takes no vengeance but to nurse
Into the happy hopelessness,
The health beyond all feeling well or ill?
Dear Robert, the basket was too heavy.
At any rate sit down and rest now.
Perhaps you'll find you still spells you
When disappointment of others passes
Who were excesses of the will only.
Perhaps you did not scatter
When flesh scattered, strained beyond flesh,
But became the you possible,
A mental body faithful
To its bodily mind.
At any rate . . . and happily . . .
For does Francisca not make light,
Keeping the open secret with a silence
As familiar as a picture
Recognized but not expected to talk?

And on the way home Robert stopped
To see if Mariana had some news
To make the day seem at least wrong –
Better a wrong day than none,
Would Robert to himself say
Before thinking wrong to be wrong.
And to try once more to mend her stove.
For Mariana Deyá is
A mildest somewhere, not more exacting
To the lazy eye than its own first glance.
Two worlds in Deyá touch.
One ends, the other starts.
And there's a going and a coming.
And a madness, time being whipped on
To reach somewhere while it's still now.
And Mariana as if America

Argues both worlds the same,
And freedom of the one no dearer bought
Than freedom of the other –
A resurrection of believing true
Whatever makes the flesh feel proud;
And the rest, that mortifies,
Called lying flesh and lying death.
Mariana for America
Argues away one world of two,
Argues away repeatedly herself,
Woman arguing herself away.
Poor Mariana. And once indeed
She heard me call her this, and railed.
'Certainty is God,' she said,
'And you are only human, like me.'
Poor Mariana, who would be human
And is thus woman argued away,
Loud and uncertain against herself,
And in her purse an emptiness
Of money wanting where truth once was –
Such generosity can but miser.
And money is her mind always
When she speaks with me too thoughtfully.
For Mariana is our landlady
Since we to Deyá and beyond came
And until Canellun is built –
House-farther-on, past place-names.

Dear Robert, and so you once again
Tried to mend Mariana's stove.
Sit down and rest now, to-day has taught you
At least to feel no new despair.
Francisca, anti-narcissus of me,
Be a fate unapparent yet half-sweet
Whom waiting may succumb to without fear
While stubborn days of will push on to death
More death-like and more natural to know.

III
How the Poem Ends

For there are still sounds of a world
As if astir where it lay dead
Not longer than a moment ago –
This very moment, now.
They have no skill in their legs to walk
Or in their heads to make up time,
And yet they quiver with old talents,
Crying up, 'Give us to do.'
But Francisca does not answer.
And glad they are not to have been heard
When they have ceased complaining
And wish for nothing but to be dead
As happily they are, and were.
Not impolitely while they murmur
Francisca sings, she does not contradict.
And such complaisance is all they want,
No second thoughts or studying.
They are but voices slow to follow
Their tongues into corruption,
And Francisca deafs me from them.
Or, honouring their poor clamour
With nicest confutation,
I'd teach them *no* in tender stages
Of their argument, then mine.
And a horror from corpse to corpse would spread,
Death tasted with too live a mind.
If they still dream the dream they dreamt
When legs and heads were human,
No need to wake them into death
Though they have overslept: the rigor takes
The body first, the mind comes of itself.
The voices will in their own time
Fall silent with embarrassment
Of having spoken false.
And Francisca intercedes till then
Between this graveyard parliament and Laura.

154

But that's enough of the world,
Never more when it was most alive
Than a cramped theatre of language –
Prophecy seemed truer than truth.
Come, to inquire wholly, not in passing.
Those are uncomfortable fashions now
Which were the world once advertised.
The too up-to-date finalities
Multiply into long ago.
Come, they have sickened and lost eloquence
And do not work their purpose, or ours.
Francisca will preside while we withdraw
To the major drama that was not meant
To be produced by their kindness
On their stage for their self-congratulation.
Francisca is a charm like a wise child
Against the childishness of the world
To be the glory-world it tells of.
She does not interrupt, obedient
To the agèd tones and gestures –
So that there's not to rage or scold
Unless upon themselves for wagging on.

Come, to leave Francisca playing
Without tossing back the ball
That rolls away, perhaps under our feet
When walking past her with this afternoon
Like to-night's cheese and lettuce in our basket,
Or spice cakes, very tough . . . to give her one. . . .
But leave her playing without looking hard.
She's at a covered game like love –
Gentle to the eye but full of hurt
That can't be helped and so better not seen.
For such a child is death at play
When the dead protest they are too young
To lie so still and be so old.

And what's the outward sign to know by
How much mortality in Deyá
On Francisca's muffling brow
Quarrels with death, then of itself is dead
More quickly than of death, and no complaining?

155

Except it is a brow more without sound
Than brows are known to be? Even mine
Yields echoes though you walk upon it
Small enough, with careful tread enough.
But Francisca's brow is perfect smoothness,
And that's the only outward sign
How still a brow it is to walk upon,
None could you ask for where to be
More left-alone, or sound of self come sooner.
The outward signs show only from within,
As Deyá from the lagging sea
Invisible or not at all appears.
The theme is mortuary
And must be so intelligenced –
By approaching land from land
And beholding with dry vision
The earthly picture, no water in the eye
To blur immediacy into vistas
Of time-hearted understanding.
For death's a now like earth on which you stand
And only readable by looking near. . . .
Which closes up the eye? Then how to see?
The eye's a weakness, gentlemen,
As you know by the delight it gives,
And never leads but it leads wrong.
And flying off to ships this way and that
You ride interpretation backwards
Until your minds-of-mariners
Are idiotic with the not-real stars.
Then there's the coming home once more.
But that's not seeing solid, only weary.
You've yet to grow short-leggèd as you were
And learn to walk without a compass.
Indeed, there's nowhere to fly off to.
Everything's here under your lashes
That you have right of knowledge in,
And what you're stupid of is stupidness. . . .
So what's the outward sign to know by
If, as I say, Francisca verily
To such and such intent . . . in Deyá . . .
Shall you perhaps take ship? see for yourself?
Francisca, here's a gentleman from life

Come all this way to meet you...
An unfriendly little girl...
A most indifferent smile for all this way....

And I? If I in Deyá am
No more envisageable phantasm
Than the problematic child, Francisca,
Then where am I, to seem a someone
In the world, filling a chair and housed
At an address that reaches me
By means of this make-believe body –
For never did I move or dwell
Outside myself – then where am I?
I lie from Deyá inward by long leagues
Of earthliness from the sun and sea
Turning inward to nowhere-on-earth.
A rumoured place? That takes us to the moon?
Let it be moon. The moon was never more
Than a name without a place to match it....
In Deyá there's a moon-blight always
On the watery irises of fancy.
And minds that feed on bodily conceits
Go daft in Deyá, especially Germans....
At any rate earth's proved, which saves
The proving of the place it gives into.
And where'd be time for that, between
Out of one, into the other, a twinkling
As fast as realizing death – or not?
Therefore, without the learned pause, to find
That Deyá is this open door I say
At least to look in by, if not to enter?

How's that? How's anything you know or don't?
You can't believe...on ordinary paper...
Printed by myself, and Robert...
He's human, by every imperfection
He's made a dogged art of....
Yes, I ink, he pulls, we patch a greyness,
Or clean the thickened letters out....*
You can't believe...do I not eat?

* This poem was first printed by hand.

With pleasure. To-day was aubergine
Browned strong in oil, and blackberries
By Robert picked and juiced into stiff jelly
Come out so good but odd.
And I eat it at all times. But eating?
That's to be kind, a madness
Executed in the stomach
But starting in the heart, which forgives.
And I forgive the idle fruits
Who have no thoughts but quick to soothe
The frowning mouths that can't agree.
And all the frightened edibles
That cringe away from argument,
Swearing they have no fixed opinion
Or ever took sides between man and –
Ah, though you can't believe, there's always God.
And that's a story you can go to sleep on
Without waking up next morning
The better or the worse for it.
Indeed, was it not written by yourselves?
A poem's by – who knows? And must be read
In prompt mistrust of the designing sense.
For once you let it have you,
There's no way out unless you leave behind
Your wits in it and wander foolish.

And so you can't believe.... And yet I speak
With a homely habit of self-pleasing
That tokens self-possession, a sure tongue?
Yes, the possession is my own.
My muse is I.... What shall we think?
The circumstances are at once
Too natural and too poetical
To determine either doubt or belief....
Let's ask Maria, she's cleaning fish
Under the algarrobas with the cats.
Her comb keeps tumbling and her cheek is shy,
But a royal manner clicks in her brain
If the question is important.
And the answer to important questions
Is of course always the same, nor long –
Another question: 'Who asks?'

Maria's wisdom is not flattering.
Perhaps she'd seem, like Queen Victoria,
A little rude, as well-bred servants are.
I'd answer you myself, but – no.
In speaking for your special sake,
Suiting the answer to the question,
My courtesy would, I fear, like hers
Be queenly, as precision is
Which otherwise were arrogance.

Let's speak to Juan White-Mule about it.
If there's a settlement between
Your certain sanity and mine,
He'll make it, and with no disrespect
To either party, a *paz mallorquina*
Founded on mutual regret
That ever did we meet to differ.
But you'd not like to pledge yourselves
To difference, owning you were
Not here when there, not right when wrong.
And I could only as usual
Linger apart in tacit presence. . . .
Sooner or later you'd strike up talk:
'Peseta's down today. What's *your* story?'
So here's my story, now let me die again
Into the stranger you can't do without,
O tourists of neighbourliness.

1931.

Index of First Lines